SURVIVAL
TRAINING AND
TECHNIQUES

JOHN MUSTON

ARMS AND ARMOUR PRESS

First published in Great Britain
in 1987 by Arms and Armour Press
Artillery House, Artillery Row, London SW1P 1RT

Reprinted 1987

Distributed in the USA by Sterling Publishing Co. Inc.,
2 Park Avenue, New York, NY 10016.

Distributed in Australia by
Capricorn Link (Australia) Pty. Ltd., P.O. Box 665,
Lane Cove, New South Wales 2066, Australia.

British Library Cataloguing in Publication Data:
Muston, John
Survival: training and techniques
1. Wilderness survival 2. Outdoor life – Safety measures
I. Title
613.6'9 GV200.5

ISBN 0-85368-811-7

Illustrations by Roy Carr.

Produced by DAG Publications Ltd.
Designed by David Gibbons; edited by Michael Boxall;
layout by Anthony A. Evans; typeset by Typesetters
(Birmingham) Ltd.

Printed and bound in Great Britain by
William Clowes Limited, Beccles and London

SURVIVAL – IMMEDIATE ACTIONS

1. Remove people from immediate danger, clear of water, avalanche, etc.

2. Render first aid. See below for priority order.

3. Stop, think and plan.

4. Start providing shelter – from wind, wet and cold.

5. Allocate jobs.

6. Put out markers, signalling devices, etc.

7. Find water and fuel.

8. Fix your position as accurately as possible.

9. Decide if, and when, you will send for help.

10. Continue all the above until found.

First Aid Priorities

Remember the key word CHASTE.

C Choking/Cardiac. Get the casualty breathing and his heart beating as quickly as possible.

H Haemorrhage. Stop major bleeding. Ignore minor cuts.

A Aid. Get others to help you and, if possible, send for an ambulance.

S Shock. Treat in the normal way.

T Treatment. Deal with other injuries, e.g., fractures, burns, etc.

E Emergency. The situation is one, so deal with it quickly and firmly.

CONTENTS

1. INTRODUCTION

This book is intended to cover the survival needs of people in the climatically temperate parts of the world, e.g., the United Kingdom and Europe. No attempt has been made to cover the specialized requirements of jungle or desert although some reference may be made to both. It does cover the problems of cold since arctic conditions can be found even in Great Britain.

With the increase in outdoor leisure pursuits such as hill-walking, sailing, camping, etc., a greater proportion of the population need to have some idea of basic survival techniques, and even those who have no intention of indulging in such activities could well find themselves in a survival situation with a broken-down car on a lonely stretch of high moorland road in the middle of winter. More than one family that has gone out onto the so-called gentle moors at the back of their home has been caught by the sudden onset of bad weather, or by a child breaking an ankle a long way from a road. No one can say 'It will never happen to me.'

More specifically this book provides a survival manual for young people in the uniformed youth organizations such as the Scouts, Girl Guides, ACF, Boys Brigade, etc. For them the outdoors should provide a large and vital part of their training programme. Not only do they need to learn and practise the skills needed for camping or climbing, but also they must know how to cope when things do not go quite as planned and they have to improvise and survive with inadequate facilities. In addition, this book caters for the needs of the young soldier in his early days in the Army when he needs to know how to defend himself not only against a possible human enemy, but also against Nature in her wilder moods.

No attempt has been made to cater for those who yearn for 'the good life' of self-sufficiency. There are no chapters on goat management or cabbage growing. The man (or woman) in a survival situation cannot wait for Nature to take its slow course with such matters. He or she is concerned with survival now.

A word of warning, especially to the younger readers. Any skill or technique needs to be practised in order to perfect it and I hope that readers will go out and do this. As a safeguard make sure your first attempt takes place within reach of civilized facilities so that you do not put yourself at risk if your first snowhole or your first attempt at improvised cooking is a disaster. If it is you will learn a lot and your next attempt will be much better. There are some things, however, you cannot practise fully. It is illegal to kill virtually all species of birds and small animals so you should not contemplate setting snares or other devices except in a real life or death situation. Only then will you have a possible excuse. Nevertheless, with the help of your friendly butcher you can certainly practise skinning and cooking a rabbit or a pigeon.

Finally, I have assumed that you have the basic knowledge to practise whatever activity you are involved in. For this reason you will not find information on how to use a compass or read a map if you are a hill-walker. Similarly, the motorist stranded on the lonely moor referred to above will not find instructions on how to change a wheel or diagnose an electrical fault. These are skills which are part of your activity interest; a lack of them may cause you to be precipitated into a survival situation so be well warned and make sure you are capable of being a safe hill-walker, competent motorist, etc.

2. A BIT OF PSYCHOLOGY:
Survival stresses

What is Survival? Before going any further it is possibly worth defining this. I suggest that the following sums it up in one not too lengthy sentence. *Survival is the art of remaining alive in and escaping from a hostile environment, without full facilities*. Something simple like that needs a bit of explanation. I, like many other mountain enthusiasts, have often camped high in some Scottish glen in the middle of winter and enjoyed it. However, I have been equipped with a good sleeping-bag, mountain tent, stove and plenty of food. That is not survival; it is winter mountain camping. At the other extreme, some backpackers and those who compete in mountain marathons and similar events pare their equipment and food down to the last fraction of an ounce – or gramme for the metrically minded – by careful selection of the lightest adequate tent, clothing, dehydrated food, etc. A total kit weight of 12lb per head is considered heavy by such people, and this includes everything needed for a weekend. Yet they will sleep warm at night and have an adequate amount of food, if not to gourmet standards. Again, that is not survival; it is lightweight camping.

In both these examples those concerned are equipped with full facilities for their chosen activity and they have planned for it. They have trained and practised, sometimes over many years, for these pastimes and have become very proficient as a result. To them the environment is not hostile; indeed, they probably gain aesthetic pleasure from being in a wild and beautiful area far from the madding crowd. To them there is no stress involved but possibly the opposite – peace and relaxation.

For another individual, clad only in a city suit and unversed in the skills of winter camping and with no specialized equipment, the same location could present a survival situation of great seriousness, in which death could well be the outcome.

WHO SURVIVES?

The answer is almost anyone. Success in a survival situation does not appear to be the preserve of any particular race, creed, sex, age group or other classification. As I write this new-born babies are being pulled out alive after being buried for nine days in the rubble of a Mexican hospital demolished by an earthquake. At the other extreme there is a well-documented case of an elderly man who broke his leg while walking alone in the Lake District but was found alive and well after 21 days. He had survived with no additional clothing or equipment other than what one might expect a hill-walker to carry for a day's walking. The babies probably survived because they were not old enough to be aware that being entombed in concrete normally causes stress. They were well wrapped in bedding and their cots protected them physically. The elderly man in the Lakes probably survived because his age brought a mature outlook to bear on the situation and because he did the maximum with the limited facilities available – a little food, a spare jersey and an understanding of the need to crawl to a sheltered spot.

Although **anyone can survive** there are indications that some qualities and characteristics will improve a person's chances of surviving. It is your mental attitude more than your ability to light a fire or carry out some other practical task which is most likely to ensure your ultimate survival. For this reason it is

FIG. 1. DETERMINATION

worth considering these qualities in some detail.

If I were allowed only one characteristic I would, without doubt, demand **determination**. This above all has kept men alive in heat, in cold, at sea, in the air, in concentration camps and in many other situations when every fibre in their body was telling them to 'Give up'. You cannot learn determination, it cannot be taken out of a bottle. It is an amalgam of your background, upbringing at home, training at school, in a youth organization or at work and, above all, what you decide to make it. It is the essential 'you' and only you can decide if, when faced with a problem, any problem, you will tackle it with everything you have got or if you will always take the easy way out and give up. In this sense, improving one's determination is easy since we can practise it every day by our approach to any problem – and life is not short of these!

Let me quote something I read in a book many years ago about a Mexican called Pablo, '. . . who survived for eight days in the desert on two gallons of water. The mean daily maximum temperature was 35°C and the mean daily minimum 28°C. Pablo's limit should have been about 50 miles; in fact, he travelled 35 miles in the saddle and at least 100 miles on foot. When Pablo was picked up his estimated weight loss was 25 per cent. His flesh was black and dry, and his lips, nose and eyelids had shrunk to nothing; his skin was covered with cuts and scratches, none of which bled. He was deaf to all but loud sounds, and blind except to light and dark, but he had retained sufficient of his faculties to find his way back almost to the camp from which he had set out. He had a slow 'roaring' respiration and a slow pulse, which could not be detected below the knees and elbows. Bad though his condition seemed, he made a complete recovery, "soaking up water like a dry sponge", then after regurgitating it at first, drinking and retaining vast quantities of water. It was three days before his vision and hearing returned to normal. Four days later he was still "deliberately and methodically devouring water-melons". One week later, a fortnight after he had been picked up, he was well, cheerful and back to his old weight, but his hair had turned grey. Pablo had been determined to live, and he succeeded.' If you can emulate Pablo you will not be lacking in determination.

Wilfred Noyce, in his book *They Survived*, examined a number of case histories of people who had experienced a major survival incident to see if there was some common thread. He found no such link, but came up with a view that soldiers/mountaineers would probably prove to be very good survivors. I must immediately declare my partiality to this view since I qualify under both counts, but Noyce, although a great mountaineer, had pacifist leanings. Nevertheless, these did not prevent his making a scholar's assessment that **self-discipline**, a trait often found in both soldiers and mountaineers, was a worthwhile quality in survival. Self-discipline makes people adopt a well-ordered lifestyle, makes them do things now rather than later, makes them do things completely and properly rather than badly and inadequately, makes them neat and tidy rather than scruffy and unkempt. Much of the daily process of living can be an exercise in self-discipline if we choose to make it so.

To survive you must be **self-sufficient.** We live in a soft, easy world with warmth and comfort available at the touch of a switch. Some lean heavily on alcohol, nicotine or other drugs for constant support. They buy their food oven-ready and their entertainment video packaged. Suddenly all this is swept away as you crawl from the crashed light aircraft or find you are forced to spend a night on a bleak mountainside. Those who have no need of these so-called aids to modern living will probably cope a lot better.

An American publication, *The Survival Book*, contains the following quote: 'Rescue Service personnel say that country boys, or city boys who have had a lot of Boy Scout training are the best survivors.' Had I not been introduced to the wonders and delights of the great outdoors as a Scout at the age of eleven I would not be writing this book or have had half a lifetime of magnificent experiences. Familiarity with **outdoor living** will provide you with the best foundation of practical skills that you could possibly want should real survival be thrust upon you. This book will give you much of the theory of survival, but it will only be of full value if you go out and practise it by getting to know Nature in all her moods as you walk, camp, climb, ski, fish, etc. In a book an igloo looks easy to build; so easy that there does not seem any point in going out to practise it on a freezing cold day when you could be watching Arsenal v. Manchester United on television. Anyway you have read somewhere that Eskimos can build one in twenty minutes so it must be easy. If you can build one in twenty minutes you should be writing this book because it takes me a lot longer – and I have practised the art.

There is no such thing as book or theoretical survival. It is an intensely practical affair when it happens. 'Knowledge Dispels Fear' is the motto of the RAF Parachute School and it is nice to remember this as you step out of the door of an aircraft 800 feet above the ground. Perhaps more importantly knowledge gives confidence. For the parachutist it is the knowledge that his parachute will open or, for the one in a million times when it does not, that he knows how to operate his reserve, which gives him the confidence to step out into space. **Confidence** in survival techniques will keep you alive for a very long time. Moreover it is the best antidote to the two great enemies of successful survival – fear and panic. More people die from wrong decisions taken as a result of panic than die from cold, heat, wild animals or other risks.

The survival of a group may well be helped by **good leadership.** This may not always come from the person with badges of rank on his arm. Some of the most unlikely people only really rise to the occasion when the need for them is totally real and vital. That rather quiet, shy person may have spent much of his life in pastimes which particularly fit him to take the lead in a survival incident. A gamekeeper or a poacher would be much more useful than a business executive if you wanted to know how to catch rabbits. It is in a survival situation that the artificial powers denoted by badges of rank or titles suddenly begin to have less impact; the leader then must lead by virtue of his personality and ability.

Physical and mental fitness will help in any survival situation. It is less likely that the overweight, out of condition man or woman will cope. There is no evidence that great bodily strength is an advantage, and there is no shortage of examples of slightly built women who have proved to be magnificent survivors. Indeed, there is a view that women, in general, will survive longer than men because of a deep-seated instinct that upon them depends the continuance of the human race. I would not dare to comment further on this theory! Mature persons, provided that they are fit, should survive more easily since they are better able to endure the sheer monotony and tedium which is part of survival. The young want to be up and doing actively when the best course of action is masterly inactivity.

MENTAL PROBLEMS OF SURVIVAL

A survival situation is a dramatic change. Very seldom indeed, does it gradually evolve. At the first hint that problems might arise in the next hour or two, people usually take avoiding action. The sailor seeing rough weather ahead sets course for a harbour or shelter. The motorist running low on fuel as he approaches a long stretch of lonely road looks for a garage and does not expect his engine to run on air when the fuel tank is empty. No one slowly breaks a leg over a number of hours. It happens in an instant, and then you are in trouble.

A sudden change of almost anything frightens people; not just the young or the old but anyone, because we all are doubtful about the unfamiliar. No one takes a large spoonful of some new foreign dish when it is first produced. We all take a small tentative taste to make sure we like it or at least can manage to get it down. If we are aware of these possible fears we will understand them when they occur and this will immediately reduce their threat by about 90 per cent. So let us consider some of the possible causes of fear. These are the more general ones, but do not forget those which are peculiar to you; like my wife, who is panic-stricken at the sight of a moth and yet thinks mice are quite friendly little things.

As I have hinted above, anything **unknown** causes a degree of apprehension. You may be a mountaineer and know the hills in all their moods and weather. To a non-mountaineer a dark brooding crag with mist swirling about it can be very frightening. Remember the first day at school? All of us have been frightened then. So much was new and unknown. You may be very frightened by your first encounter with the jungle, but just stop and remember that thousands of people live all their lives in the jungle and do it very well. Thousands more from Western civilizations have, over the centuries, gone into the jungle, explored it, exploited it and survived quite happily – and so could you. You just stop, take a few deep breaths, then start thinking and planning. The unknown soon becomes the known and familiar. You were once new in the place where you live and it was all unknown. Now you probably know it like the proverbial back of your hand.

Few of us seek out **discomfort** for the sake of it. Some of us put up with it in order to enjoy some greater pleasure. To climb a high mountain will, almost certainly, involve some discomfort, but the reward in the view at the top or the sense of achievement makes the discomfort worth enduring. I am told (you will appreciate that this is something I cannot test for myself) that there is some discomfort in childbirth, but I have yet to meet a mother who counted it but a small thing in comparison with the wonder and thrill of the new-born baby. Despite these examples generally we do not enjoy discomfort and for some, especially those who take care never to stray far from soft beds, warm rooms and mechanized travel, it is a matter for real fear. The thought of being cold, wet, hungry, etc., is a major worry; yet one of the great sayings of the outdoorsman is 'any fool can be uncomfortable' implying that one can be comfortable with very little. An experienced camper will always make himself very comfortable. A little practise and experience of the outdoors will solve this problem for you for ever.

Most of us are with **people** every day and yet we can fear them especially in the unusual circumstances of survival. At arm's length in normal life we are happy with most people, but huddled together in a tiny snowhole is a different matter. You may think that you are God's gift to the opposite sex, but the reverse is probably much nearer the truth; so think about how you can minimize other people's fears of you. Kindness, courtesy and a caring attitude will go a long way to alleviate the fears of others, and what better place to start than in your everyday life. If you have fear of others you must hope that they will have read this book and be trying to help you. But look for their better qualities and try to see them as ordinary people like you despite the colour of their skin, their accent, their style of dress or whatever else it is that frightens you.

In a difficult situation we are often frightened that our **own weaknesses** will let us down. In an expensive restaurant we worry about which of the imposing array of knives, forks and spoons to use for which course. In a survival situation we will worry that we will not be able to keep up, or keep a fire going when it is our turn. The solution is to practise survival skills under controlled conditions so that you are familiar with them if you ever need them for real. If you have not trained yourself in this way beforehand, take heart from the fact that possibly most of those with you will not know any more than you. If any people in the group claim to be experts, let them show the

rest of you what to do. Remember, the one thing an expert likes to do is show how good an expert he really is. If he is only a 'mouth expert' his lack of ability will soon show up and that will put him right back along with the rest of you. No matter how inexpert you think you are you can do something, maybe only one thing, better than everyone else. Someone I know acted as leader to a party of people on a package tour to see some of the natural wonders of Iceland and this included travelling in a tracked vehicle over the snowfields. The weather got rough and my friend had finally to ski ahead to find the route. One of the party was an American lady of very ample proportions who was quite hopeless at everything. One night, however, when they camped it was very cold and the butter was rock-solid and difficult to use. This lady said, 'Give it to me,' and enfolded the block of butter somewhere in the inner recesses of her clothing and within a short time the butter was in a perfect state for spreading. Even she had one thing she could do well.

I have briefly mentioned **terrain and climate** in the introduction to this section. Most of us live in cities and we enjoy the temperate climate of Europe, but remember that people dwell all over the world in all sorts of environments and weather conditions. For some the starker places of the earth such as the desert or the Arctic are sought out as places of beauty. They feel wonderfully at home there and so can you if you realize that you can live anywhere if you make a few small adjustments to your style of living. In the tropics people get up early and take a rest in the middle part of the day, working again in the evening if necessary. If you are suddenly precipitated into a new environment, just stop, look around and take an interest in what is different about it. Then think and plan how you are going to cope.

If I were to ask you when you were last completely **alone** for a period of more than 24 hours I am sure you would find it difficult to recall. You may live alone in your own house or flat, but very few of us work totally alone and even fewer never go shopping, have a drink in a pub or go somewhere where they come into contact with other humans. Even a lighthouse-keeper on the most isolated of lights is one of a team of three or four men. If you are forced into a survival situation you could well be on your own and that can be very frightening. Man is a gregarious animal and all his instincts are to be with others be it as part of a family, in a work group, in a sports team or whatever it may be. The recluse or hermit is considered a very odd sort of person and is himself sometimes feared because he is not quite normal. The character Robinson Crusoe was based on the actual experiences of Alexander Selkirk who did survive alone on a desert island. Trappers on the north-east coast of Greenland used to spend the entire winter alone apart from a dog team as they visited their traplines. Overcoming fear is a matter of gaining self-confidence in your ability to cope with any situation and you can, of course, experience being totally alone by going off for a few days' camping in some remote area like the Highlands of north-west Scotland. With experience and with plenty to occupy youself, being on your own ceases to be a problem. Alexander Selkirk and the Greenland trappers coped and so can you.

In the paragraphs above I have drawn your attention to some of the most common fears that are likely to assail you when forced into a survival situation. The knowledge that you will almost certainly, to a greater or lesser extent, suffer these fea.s is the best antidote to their effect. I have briefly suggested ways of alleviating the fears still further. The greak risk is that you will let fear so take control of you that you will no longer be in command of the situation. Then you will panic and start taking wrong decisions and initiat-

ing the wrong actions. If you begin to be frightened, stop, sit down and think for a while. Think about something totally different, and avoid taking any decisions until you have calmed down and are thinking rationally once more. Now I want to describe some of the material stresses that could face you.

PHYSICAL PROBLEMS OF SURVIVAL

Cold and heat are two ends of the same problem. Man is basically a tropical animal. In other words, for him to exist without some form of protective clothing he needs to be within a few degrees north or south of the Equator. Try spending 24 hours in Great Britain clad in nothing but a swimming-costume and you will soon decide that clothing, especially the warm sort, is a very good idea. If you go out for a winter day in the Scottish hills properly clad in the recommended clothing and are then forced to spend a night out with no additional clothing, sleeping-bag, etc., you will survive but I doubt if you will describe the night as comfortable. In temperate regions extreme heat will seldom be a problem unless you have a delicate skin or complexion. In the tropics it can kill you; and in a few hours unless you take very careful precautions. For survival you will never be able to select the ideal degree of heat or cold; you will be in it whatever it may be. The human body can survive a very wide range of temperatures, depending obviously on the availability of clothing, shelter, etc. Two friends of mine spent a night out at 28,000 feet on Everest, in a hole scraped in the snow and without sleeping-bags. The temperature was probably between $-30°$ and $-40°C$. They suffered from frostbite but they survived. At the other extreme people have survived temperatures of over 60°C. Extremes of temperature will cause stress but you can survive them.

Precipitation, be it rain, snow, hail or sleet, will in itself be little problem, unless it is associated with wind as in a blizzard. It is the secondary effect of rain-soaked clothing or cold which will cause the discomfort and, therefore, stress. Other than as a source of water, precipitation does you no good so should be avoided as far as possible by the use of protective clothing or other shelter.

Solar radiation is mainly a problem at high altitude, in places like the European Alps, especially when associated with snow-covered ground which reflects the sun's rays. However it can affect some people at sea level on a very hot sunny day, and sunburn causes discomfort and stress. The golden rule for survival is that you never sunbathe and you keep most of your skin, other than the weathered parts, covered at all times. Even the face may need some protection at sea level and it certainly will at high altitude.

Most people think that **hunger** is the thing to be most feared and that without eating you will die in a few days. Nothing could be further from the truth. Your stomach tells you, usually three times a day, that it wants food and you appease it by having a meal. While a feeling of hunger is mildly unpleasant it does, in fact, disappear after about four days with nothing to eat. Perhaps the stomach gives the whole thing up as a bad job and stops being difficult! In recent times we have had Irishmen on hunger-strikes and they survived for more than sixty days before dying. It might be argued that they had a death-wish rather than a determined will to survive, which is what I hope you have. A girl named Helen Klaben was a passenger in a light aircraft flying down the west coast of North America. It crashed in a wild, remote area and she and the pilot were not found for forty-nine days. Both were in quite good shape, having had little more than a packet of sandwiches and some berries to sustain them for all that time in weather which was below freezing.

You will die of **thirst** long before you die of hunger. In temperate climates you can last about fifteen days without any water at all. For every litre of water you have you should survive an extra day, so plan your water rationing accordingly. In hot climates the water needs of the human body rise dramatically. This will be dealt with more fully in a later chapter.

Shock will occur to some member of a survival party in almost every instance. It may be shock in the first-aid sense, which always occurs with any injury, or the shock to anyone finding himself in a dramatically different situation. Warmth, reassurance and confidence building are the proven treatment for shock and it is important to remember that all are likely to suffer from it to some extent in the immediate aftermath of any incident.

Motion sickness can produce considerable stress especially in those who suffer badly, and a small liferaft or life-boat provides a lot of movement. Most of these craft have first-aid kits fitted and these include suitable tablets to lessen the effect of the motion. There is no virtue in being 'tough' or 'brave' and not taking such tablets. Sea-sickness produces dehydration and, almost certainly, you will have very little water to replace fluids lost by vomiting so anything you can do to minimize the loss of fluids will prolong your life.

Gas poisoning can occur with any sort of stove or combustion engine. All can produce carbon monoxide which is fatal to humans. Because it is colourless and odourless the risk is enhanced compared to butane gas supplied for camping stoves which incorporates a stenching agent to make an escape of gas from the cylinder very obvious. Adequate ventilation even in the worst weather is the only solution.

Wild animals, even quite small ones, are a major worry in the mind of the city-bred layman. Although Richard Attenborough and others have brought wildlife into our sitting-rooms by way of the television screen, the average person is not familiar with them in real life. The wild places of the world are not teeming with animals just waiting for a meal of juicy human. Most animals keep well away from all humans and since they will be aware of you long before you are aware of them your chances of having more than a fleeting glimpse are remote. Despite several years spent in wild and remote country I have virtually no good photographs of animals; the pictures you see in magazines and books are usually the result of waiting for days or weeks in a hide near a watering-place or where bait has been put out. Even then, telephoto lenses have to be used to get those close-up shots we all like. You must avoid putting temptation in the way of animal marauders by leaving food out. One of the big problems in the American national parks is where to put your food so that it does not attract bears. Usually it is hung high in a tree suspended in a bag from a rope, but I have read that the bears are learning how to get at the food even then. All food remnants such as fish and animal bones should be deposited a long way from your shelter area. Food preparation should be done by a stream which will wash remnants away. The rule is to do nothing to encourage animals and never to interfere with them. A female will defend her young very fiercely and this accounts for the majority of animal attacks on humans.

A few insects such as mosquitoes, lice, etc., can be dangerous for the diseases they carry, and the best protection is full body cover of clothing with the cuffs of sleeves and the bottoms of trousers drawn tight to stop them penetrating. Some, such as midges and blackfly, can drive people almost mad with their attentions as anyone who has camped in Scotland in July or August can testify. They cause no harm except irritation. If you have some form of anti-midge repellant use it. Failing that, total coverage of the body by clothing or some form of tentage is the only answer. A pipeful of some especially noxious

shag tobacco is also useful to keep the bugs at bay.

One or more members of a party sustaining **severe injuries** will add stress to the situation. Obviously the casualties themselves will suffer stress and shock as a concomitant to their injuries, but the fit members will also feel some degree of stress. Will they survive? What happens if we have to move? How can we take them with us? Will this mean we cannot escape? What happens if they die? This last, is without being too callous, the easiest problem. If a casualty does die all you can do is place the body reverently in some quiet spot until such time as rescue arrives. If this is likely to be more than a few hours, a shallow grave or in a rock mound if ground is frozen is the answer. However, you must do all in your power to treat injuries or illness with whatever facilities you have. As far as possible your treatment should comply with what you have learned in first aid training (you have done some, haven't you?) about clean dressings, hygiene, etc. But those teachings must never overrule life-saving treatment. If the only available absorbent material is your grubby handkerchief, use it to stop major bleeding. If a few bugs get into the wound, that is far better than bleeding to death. Do remember also that most wounds look far worse than they are. Blood is only a red, slightly sticky liquid, and will do no harm to you so get on with the treatment and have no thoughts of fainting or being sick. Practise by watching a few medical programmes – in full colour – on the television, then perhaps the sight of a bit of blood will not worry you too much.

We live in a sanitized world of flush lavatories, sweet-smelling soap, frequent showers and clean clothes. In the wild there is a total **lack of sanitation.** If the calls of nature have to be satisfied behind a tiny clump of heather or in the middle of a totally bare glacier this will cause embarrassment to many who are not used to such coarse living. The lack of clean clothes or the chance of a good wash will affect the morale of many people especially after the first fortnight. I am not advocating that no attempt be made to maintain the highest possible standards of personal hygiene. The concern for such standards is a vital part of the whole survival process, but it is important to realize that even the best attempt to maintain standards will, in some circumstances be low compared to what most people are used to in civilized society. Oddly enough, despite our concern for cleanliness, little harm will come to you if you do not wash. The Tibetans have been proving this for centuries! In time you are likely to acquire fleas, lice, etc., depending on where you are, but they affect our sense of dignity rather than our bodily well-being. By all means try to keep yourself clean, but do not worry or fuss if you cannot. Ultimately those soft towels and hot water will seem all the more attractive.

If you are forced into a survival situation suddenly at any altitude over about 6,000 feet you could suffer from **lack of oxygen.** Most people will not suffer until they are above 12,000 feet and then only if they try to move quickly or energetically. It is important, if you are at altitude, to move very slowly and carefully at least for the first few days until you acclimatize. Himalayan mountaineers rightly lay much stress on slow and steady acclimatization before they attempt any high peak. After an aircraft crash, for example, you may

FIG. 2. SURVIVAL IS A STRESSFUL AFFAIR!

find yourself suddenly on very high mountains and have to cope with the splitting headaches, nausea, vomiting that can be caused. If at all possible descend to a lower altitude. Apart from reducing the risk of oedema – excess fluid in the lungs, brain or peripheral parts of the body – caused by being high up, you will also be warmer, nearer fuel, food and civilization in general.

SURVIVAL LEADERSHIP

In this chapter so far I have tried to outline and explain most of the fears and stresses which are likely to assail anyone suddenly projected into a survival problem. Coping fully with these is the most important thing of all. For you, a person who is interested in these things, the solution is fairly simple. Read this chapter again and make sure you realize what the fears and stresses are likely to be. Knowledge of them will go a long way to overcoming them. Next, consider how you would deal with them. You may have better ideas than those I have suggested. Follow this with training yourself in all the practical details of survival described in later chapters of this book. With this training you will gain a tremendous amount of confidence to deal with *any* survival situation you may find yourself in.

But what if you find yourself in a situation with a lot of other people; hysterical children, grown men in a total funk? You may not think you are the person to take control; you may have great inner doubts that you can do it, but it may well be that you will be the most suitable and experienced person because no one else will have thought about survival except you. You will have read about it and practised it. Every time you go into a building you notice, almost subconsciously, possible escape routes in case of fire. Flying to a holiday overseas you do not just think what a good figure the stewardess has got, but listen carefully to her when she describes the emergency exits during the pre-flight briefing. On a mountain walk you put as much effort into planning possible escape routes, for use if the weather turns bad, as into the main route for the day. Because you live survival you are almost certainly the one to take charge so make no excuses – get on with it.

If you are in a uniform; any uniform be it police, military, Scout or any other, that is a bonus. Frightened people will respond to instructions from such a person and they will not bother whether the person has any badges of rank. At first you may well have to raise your voice to get some quiet and order. Later you should be able to use a quiet but firm approach. A loud 'Stop that row at once!' to someone crying noisily should reduce the decibels. I leave the possible selection of adjectives to you. For a serious hysterical case you may have to say it several times or, as a last resort, slap the hysteric's face. Having gained some measure of control the next priority is to get everyone involved in a task so that they have less time to think about themselves and their predicament. The fit can comfort and treat the injured, others can start gathering, for example, wood for a fire, sections of aircraft to use for shelter, suitcases, etc.

Do not chase or harry people but keep them occupied. Only get involved yourself if there is a clear need for personal leadership – usually for a particularly unpleasant task. For the most part you should be thinking and planning what to do next. Activity reduces stress in people, but once the situation is under control have regular breaks for a rest, or a hot drink if it is possible. Let people have a laugh and a joke; a sense of humour is a very valuable thing in a difficult situation. After the initial few hours you should establish a routine. While hoping for early rescue you, at least, should plan on having to survive for day, maybe weeks. It is you that will have to keep a routine going and encourage those who get depressed. Change duties round so that the same people are not always doing the same chores. Encourage people to conserve their resources, both personal and material, and waste nothing. Not only should every scrap of food be consumed, but extra care should be taken of clothing, keeping it dry and as clean as possible. No one can have too much sleep and they should conserve their body heat as far as possible by not standing around getting cold. A sleeping-bag or other protection is not something to be in only from eleven at night to seven in the morning. If in doubt – rest!

Some people have the ability to switch off from their surroundings and bury themselves in a book. Others may prefer to talk, but try to keep them off morbid discussion of the survival chances and similar topics. Right from the start you or someone deputed by you should keep a diary of events. It is an ideal role for someone who is injured and cannot play a full part in other survival activities. A strong religious faith has proved immensely helpful to many who have been in the most appalling situations, and a person with such faith can prove a great strength and support. You may not have that faith and it cannot be learned, but an American polar survival expert has written 'Many men who have never met the Almighty in church, meet Him occasionally at the operating or delivery table, but really get to know Him at the ends of the earth.' Your survival situation will be an 'end of the earth' and people will appreciate time being made for a simple service or a few prayers on a daily basis. It will be a wonderful help to most of those with you. I would strongly advocate that part of your study of and training for survival should be to find out more about your religious faith so that it becomes more real. For the past thirty years I have found my own Christian faith a wonderful support in all aspects of life, but even more so at times of great difficulty. Let me relate one personal experience.

In the summer of 1972 I led an expedition to Axel Heiberg Island in Arctic Canada. For seven weeks we climbed, sledged and explored in mainly good weather, but at the end as the various parties were coming down to base camp to fly out the weather turned very nasty. Of the last party of four only two struggled back to camp. There had been an accident with one person killed and another injured who had had to be left up on a glacier in a tent. Clearly the rest of us had to mount a rescue and I, as the expedition leader, had to organize it but my mind was in a turmoil. What should we take? How would we find the casualty? What equipment did we need? Suddenly I knew I should commit the whole problem to God in prayer and I bowed my head and prayed for a few seconds. My mind cleared and without any shadow of doubt I knew what we needed to do, to take and so on. After a good meal we set off. Navigation was difficult in the thick mist and we were too near the Magnetic North Pole for the compass to be much use. Several times we went wrong but always found our bearings again. After about ten hours we were all very tired, our clothing was frozen and we were lost once more. I knew that a second problem was looming. How long before the rescue party themselves might need help? How long before they might succumb to hypothermia? Again I prayed and had a strong feeling that we should go on for another half-hour before turning back to wait for good weather. About twenty minutes later we came to an oddly-shaped bollard of ice which we had passed many times before and we knew precisely where we were. An hour or two later we were with the casualty. We prepared him for evacuation and after nearly 24 hours out we were all safely back at base camp. If you are a cynic you will say that my service background had trained me to deal with a crisis and come to the right decisions, but only I know the total change which came over me after committing the problems to prayer on those two occasions.

Let me remind you of the priorities of immediate action in an emergency:

1. Remove people from immediate danger.
2. Render first aid.
3. Stop, think and plan.
4. Provide shelter – from wind, wet and cold.
5. Allocate jobs.
6. Put out markers, signalling devices, etc.
7. Find water and fuel.
8. Fix your position as accurately as possible.
9. Decide if, and when, you will send for help.
10. Continue all the above until found. You as the leader need to keep going over these priorities again and again.

Survival is 110, not 100 per cent concentration and attention to detail. Always ask 'How can I improve the situation?' Have I done everything possible? You never say 'I can't be bothered,' or 'What's the point?' Survival is a mental discipline and it needs determination and confidence. You can survive if you want to. You must never, ever give up.

3. MAN IS A TROPICAL ANIMAL:
Warmth and shelter

CLOTHING

Had he not been blessed with sufficient intelligence to provide clothing and shelter for himself, *homo sapiens* would have been one of the animals only found in tropical areas. He (and she) has virtually no hair, fur or feathers to keep the body warm. Even the fattest person is poorly provided with insulating fat compared to, for example, the blubber layer of a seal. The polar bear happily swims in the Arctic Ocean at all times of the year with no ill effect, yet man would succumb in a matter of minutes in such waters. The secret is the insulation of the main part of the body from the cold outside. In cold weather birds, when they are not flying look fatter than usual. This is because they have the ability to fluff up their feathers, especially the small down feathers close to the skin, to increase the insulating layer thickness. At the onset of winter, animals grow a thicker layer of fur to protect them through the coming cold months. Making the best use of the clothing you have available provides you with a micro-climate all of your own in the inch or two around your body. In the ideal situation this micro-climate will keep you comfortable – not too hot and not too cold. However survival is seldom ideal.

If you take part in outdoor activities such as climbing or sailing your choice of suitable clothing for such pastimes will be governed by the fact that you will often have to protect yourself from the cold or the wet. If you wait for a perfect fine day before you go on the hills you will do very little mountaineering indeed. It is accepted good practice for all outdoor activities that you wear or carry clothing and equipment to cope with the worst conditions you are likely to encounter. Should you then become involved in a survival situation you have appropriate clothing with you, but what about the non-outdoor type or the outdoor person driving from A to B who runs into trouble? His clothing is likely to owe more to fashion or accepted standards of status or work. The same principles apply even if the end result is less satisfactory than would be obtained from garments designed specifically for rugged conditions. The American forces have an appropriate mnemonic 'COLD' as an aid to remembering how to use clothing to the best. Although it is designed to help you keep warm in cold weather most of the advice applies to keeping cool in hot weather.

Keep clothing	**C**lean
Avoid	**O**verheating
Wear clothing	**L**oose and in **L**ayers
Keep clothing	**D**ry

In survival conditions you will have no washing-machine, probably no soap and possibly limited water. Despite this you should keep clothing as clean as conditions and facilities allow. Dirty clothing becomes matted and the tiny spaces between the fibres cannot trap as much air as before and it is this trapped air which is the secret of insulation. Oil from the body also fills these tiny spaces. On the outside layer of clothing a film of dirt gradually builds up as we go about the chores in our survival location. Getting firewood, or digging turf to roof a shelter will soon make outer garments dirty. As far as your survival activities allow, keep clean. Do not be hidebound by convention. You may only have one pair of underpants but nothing will happen if you take them off, wash them and then have to do without them for a few hours while they dry. What mother may have told you is not always right when life gets rugged.

For various reasons it is important to avoid overheating. You should make a deliberate effort to carry out your survival chores slowly and steadily. This will conserve every bit of your available energy and it should stop you sweating. Moisture is a poor insulator and so sweat-soaked garments do not insulate you as well as dry ones. Sweating is part of the body mechanism to keep the body cool. Evaporation of sweat cools the body because body heat is used to change the sweat from a liquid state to a gaseous state. So again you are not helping yourself to keep warm. In cold conditions you should aim to feel slightly cold rather than too warm. Sweating produces various chemicals which are absorbed by the clothing thus making them dirty which again reduces their insulation value. When any active work is done clothing should be loosened or removed to prevent any overheating. Whether you are wearing specialized outdoor clothing or garments more suited to city streets the same principles apply. Avoid overheating and you will be cleaner and warmer.

For warmth all clothing should be loose fitting and in several thin layers rather than a few thick layers. An early part of your Survival – Immediate Actions should be to check and loosen any tight clothing. In extreme cases it could be better to remove it. Tight shoe-laces or anorak cuffs will certainly give you cold hands and feet and could, in severe conditions, cause frostbite. Ties, belts and underwear should all be loosened. No matter how ample her bust-line a lady will come to no harm if she slackens off her bra fastenings. There should be nothing to restrict the flow of blood around the body. An unrestricted flow keeps you warm and stops frost-bite. Loose clothing traps pockets of air between the layers. Tight clothing, such as a pair of jeans, only provides insulation of the thickness of the garment material, usually no more than a frac-

tion of an inch. Loose clothing allows perhaps half an inch of trapped air over at least part of the body. Several thin layers rather than one thick layer increases the possibility of these pockets of air and allows much greater flexibility in the amount of clothing worn. Because the blood flows near the surface of much of the head there is proportionally a great loss of heat (about 20 per cent) from there compared to other parts of the body. Some form of head covering, even improvised, should always be worn to reduce this. Additional clothing might be improvised from old sacking, large polythene bags, etc., with grass or leaves used as insulation.

Clothing made damp by sweating has been covered above, but clothing can also become wet from rain or snow. Unless the rain is prolonged it is usually better to find shelter and wait for dry conditions before continuing your survival actions. Snow should be frequently brushed off outer garments before it has a chance to melt and penetrate clothing. It is especially important to remove all snow before entering any sort of shelter that you may have improvised. If clothing does get wet you should get it dry as soon as possible. If it is soaking wet, e.g., from falling in a river, it must be hung up and you must hope for what a housewife would call 'a good drying day'. Alternatively you may be able to dry it by a fire, but beware of sparks and flames damaging your very limited stock of clothing. A few years ago I got ashore from a swamped rubber boat onto Ruth Island in the Inner Fjord area of East Greenland. We soon had a fire going with driftwood and draped our clothing and equipment round it. Later we discoverd that while perforations are a good thing in teabags they are not good in a down-filled sleeping-bag. Garments which are only damp, e.g., a sweaty vest, should be removed, a dry layer such as a jersey put on next to the skin and the damp garment put on over that. A combination of body heat and air drying should solve the problem in an hour or two.

Whether you are a city type or an outdoor type I suggest that at least some of your clothing should be bought with survival in mind. Let me suggest the sort of garments you might buy. Stout boots or shoes will always serve you better than some fancy fashion shoe with pointed toes. The ideal socks would be fairly thick wool or loop stitched synthetic fibre. For the trunk and limbs you need clothing that will trap as much air in the fibres as possible. Wool sweaters, fibrepile garments, wool/cotton mixture shirts are all very satisfactory. Underclothes made from 100 per cent polypropylene have the property of 'wicking' away sweat from the skin and thus avoiding that clammy feeling you get from a sweat-soaked vest or shirt. Any of these materials are also suitable for gloves, mitts and head covering. Nevertheless, no matter how good any of these insulating garments are, their value will be largely lost if they are not covered by a windproof layer. Quite a mild wind of ten or fifteen knots will soon be felt through any of these insulating garments if they are not covered with a jacket or anorak of closely woven cotton or polycotton.

Various trade names such as 'Ventile' and 'Grenfell Cloth' are advertised, but

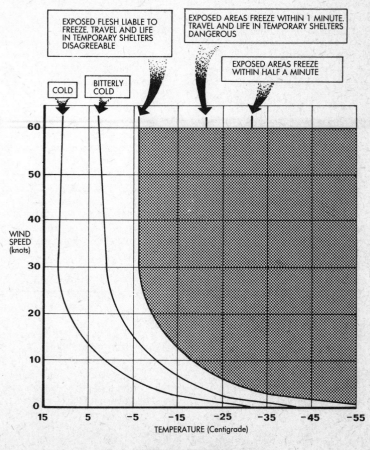

FIG. 3. A SIMPLIFIED WINDCHILL GRAPH

the basic material is a very good quality and tightly woven cotton. An alternative is to have an outer layer of waterproof clothing. Any waterproof garment is also windproof, but until recently this sort of clothing had the disadvantage of causing condensation to form on the inside of the garment as soon as any appreciable activity took place. This condensation transferred itself to the jersey or shirt and the process of losing insulation began. From a survival point of view the advantage of this moisture is that it is warm wet rather than the killing cold wet of penetrating rain. Recent developments in fabrics have produced what are known as 'breathables' which to a varied extent keep out raindrops but allow the passage of water vapour from the body through microscopic pores in the waterproof layer. Goretex is currently the best fabric for this, but any purchase should be preceded by discussion with a reputable retailer. Oiled cotton, and neoprene-proofed garments are satisfactory, but I cannot recommend polyurathene-proofed clothing for use in heavy or prolonged rain. For survival purposes the design of such garments is not critical, but a hood is vital and a full-length zip very useful since it allows flexibility in avoiding overheating. Beyond that it is a matter of personal choice. Your overall aim with clothing should be to keep wind, precipitation and cold out and your body heat in to maintain a comfortable micro-climate in which to exist. The simplified windchill graph at Figure 3 shows that a person in a 50-knot wind at 11°C is as much at risk as a person at minus 14°C but with only a 2-knot wind. Do not underestimate the danger of wind when in the great outdoors.

SHELTERS

Even if a person in a survival situation is fortunate enough to have plenty of clothing and/or a survival bag suitable for the climate he is in, there are good reasons to provide some form of additional shelter. First, it will provide yet more shelter from the elements than the clothing. In difficult circumstances you can never have too much protection and it is a lucky man, indeed, who can discard insulation because he is too warm when at rest. A shelter will bring members of a group together and there is much strength to be gained from one another in difficult circumstances. In strictly practical terms real warmth can be gained from a group of people who huddle together. The human body constantly radiates the heat of a 100-watt light bulb. While you should do all you can – see the discussion on clothing above – to reduce the heat radiated, some will inevitably escape. It is much better that this heat be passed to those with you rather than being lost to the atmosphere, so the closer you can get to your survival companions the better. The less surface area the body exposes the better since there is less heat loss, so never stand around in the open unless you have some task to carry out. Get into shelter and fold yourself up into a ball. To encourage you to do this keep any shelter small. Even if you have the materials do not build a palace. Any shelter should be just big enough for the party to sit and lie in comfort, but only just. The air in the shelter then heats up more quickly and keeps its heat more easily. The shelters illustrated in this book are the ideal, but you will seldom achieve this. The ground will be different or the best materials will not be available. The important thing is to grasp the principles and then modify the design to the location in which you find yourself.

NATURAL MATERIALS SHELTERS

The simplest shelter is a cave. It is often ready for use apart from removing the odd stone from the floor. Caves are not always dry, but usually some part of them will be better than trying to cope outside. A large rock or boulder, especially if it is overhanging, will offer some immediate shelter and you can soon improve it by building a stone wall or sangar round it – see Figure 4. A fold or a dip in the ground can also be the start of a shelter and you can improve it as time and available materials allow – see Figure 5. The gaps between the stones can be filled in with lumps of turf or heather to make an airtight windbreak. With a dry stone wall construction the problem of providing a roof remains. If any timber can be found it can be used as rafters and large flat stones laid across to form a flat or sloping roof. If you are trying to survive in wooded country the problem of a shelter is much easier. Figure 6 shows a simple one- or two-man shelter made from a framework of timbers with

foliage as the roof. Many materials such as bracken, the foliage branches of pine trees or even large leaves like those from wild rhubarb can be used; if you have some sheeting, use it. The important thing is to start the thatching process at ground level and then fix on the overlapping layers progressively towards the top of the shelter. Notice how tiles are positioned on a house in order to shed the rain. Remember also that there must be plenty of overlap to reduce the risk of leaks. Figure 7 shows another sort of shelter commonly called a lean-to. Because of the large open side this is only suitable if you have such a plentiful supply of wood that you can keep a good fire going night and day. With such a fire the back of the shelter acts as a reflector to the heat and so warms your back as well. In Figure 7 I have shown another smaller reflector on the other side of the fire to make it even cosier. I have purposely left out dimensions because the size of a shelter will vary according to the number of people to be accommodated. A cave might well take twenty whereas a brushwood-type shelter can only take about four. Above this number you are better dividing into two or more parties and building additional shelters. If you can, keep the size of a shelter to the minimum possible for very modest

FIG. 4. AN IMPROVED BOULDER

FIG. 5. AN IMPROVED FOLD IN THE GROUND

FIG. 6. A ONE- OR TWO-MAN SHELTER (TWO VARIATIONS)

FIG. 7. A LEAN-TO

FIG. 8. TREE TRUNK SHELTER (BEFORE THATCHING OVER THE FRAME)

comfort; it will give you a chance to get to know people better than ever before! The trunk of a large fallen tree could provide a shelter for a very modest amount of additional work. Figure 8 gives an idea of how to do this.

If you are forced to survive in snow-covered terrain you are probably better off, apart from the lower temperature, than in a more temperate climate. Snow can be cut and shaped, within certain limits, to whatever you want it to do. The simplest and quickest shelter is what I call a snow grave, but since survival is a positive thinking affair most people call it a snow trench. Figure 9 shows that it is a simple trench cut in the snow. If the snow is in the right condition you can cut the roofing blocks from the trench as shown. However snow is not always, especially in the United Kingdom, suitable to cut easily into blocks; it frequently just crumbles. Try digging down through the surface layer and you may find more consolidated snow, but be prepared to find none that will remain in block form. Even without a roof a snow trench achieves a lot since you are below the surface and so out of the wind. In the absence of snow blocks any sort of sheet will make a good flat roof provided it is well weighted with snow or rocks. One big advantage of the snow trench is that it can be dug in very flat areas. Normally it need only be about eighteen inches deep and 20 to 25 minutes should see the finished article. Some years ago two of us dug one in this time just off the summit of Cairngorm in Scotland during a course run by Glenmore Lodge. Despite a lack of sleeping-bags it was with some reluctance that we emerged at midnight when the instructor relented and allowed the course to return to the comforts of the Lodge. We were quite snug and could not only have survived until morning, but we would have been in a fit state to carry out a normal day's mountain walking. What sort of shelter is possible depends to a certain extent on the tools you have or can improvise. Both the snow trench and the snow cave can be dug with just an ice axe and nothing more, although any sort of improvised shovel would make it easier.

Figure 10 shows the general design of a snow cave. I have managed to dig a one-man version in about 90 minutes with just an ice axe and a plate as a scoop and I doubt that one, irrespective of its size, could be dug in much less. Depending on the snow conditions and the size of the snow drift it is possible to dig very large caves holding as many as twenty people, but these tend to be dug as planned living accommodation rather than for survival use. The basic requirement is a snowdrift of well-con-

(A)

(B)

FIG. 9. SNOW TRENCH — (A) USING SNOW BLOCKS, (B) USING A SHEET FOR A ROOF

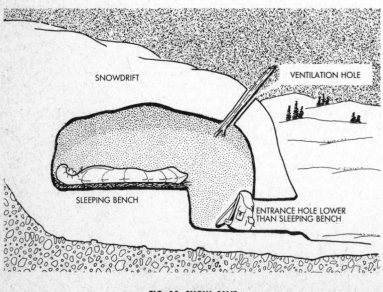

SNOWDRIFT

VENTILATION HOLE

SLEEPING BENCH

ENTRANCE HOLE LOWER
THAN SLEEPING BENCH

FIG. 10. SNOW CAVE

solidated snow at least eight feet deep both horizontally and vertically. Greater depth is even better. Before starting to dig you should put on waterproofs if you have them since it is a damp procedure. Tunnel horizontally into the drift and only begin to hollow out the cave when you are sure you have at least eighteen inches of good consolidated snow above you. Whether you hollow out to the left, to the right or straight ahead is a matter of choice *and* the shape of the ground under the snow. You may well hit a boulder. You just have to work round such an obstacle, but it does mean that few snow caves actually end up like the nice neat drawings used to show their design. How you improve your home from home is up to you. For basic survival, especially if you or your party are at the end of your tether, a simple cave is probably all you can manage, but as time goes on you may hollow out sleeping-bays, a cooking shelf or even a latrine. Figure 11 shows a design for a really de luxe cave for a large party of survivors. While such a design will require many manhours of work it is worth remembering, especially if you are the leader of a surviving party, that time may hang heavy after the initial

activity of establishing your camp, and it will be a good therapeutic activity to get the party improving their living conditions. It will be good for their morale and self-esteen but do not tell them this!

Whatever the design there are certain basic features which are critical. First, the entrance must be at the lowest point of the whole construction thus ensuring that warm air is retained as far as possible. The sleeping-shelf should be as high as possible for the same reason. You need only enough room to lie on it in modest comfort. Secondly, ventilation is vital. Make sure you have a ventilation hole which is kept clear especially if snow is drifting heavily outside. The entrance can be filled with a snow block or a filled rucksack. You will find that even if there is a howling blizzard outside, all is quiet in the cave. Combined with lack of oxygen, this will make you less aware of any lack of ventilation. This particularly applies if you are cooking with a possible buildup of carbon monoxide. For this reason you should always cook near the entrance. Thirdly, the internal roof of the cave should be domed and smooth. This will ensure that any water formed will run down the dome to the sides rather than drip in the middle of the

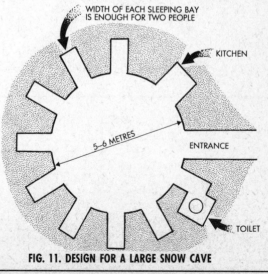

FIG. 11. DESIGN FOR A LARGE SNOW CAVE

cave. Smooth off all small projections on the dome. Additionally you may need small drainage channels round your sleeping or cooking areas. Fourthly, make sure you site your cave in a safe place where there is no risk of avalanche, stone fall, etc. Externally the entrance should be marked with a stick of some sort which needs to be as long as possible; quite an amazing amount of drifting can take place overnight and a cave entrance can easily be buried to a depth of some feet. Finally, remember to take all your equipment, food, etc., into the cave at night. Drifting snow can mean the loss of vital items. You should always have close at hand some sort of digging implement to get out in a hurry if need be. Remove all loose snow from your clothing before entering and keep any wet clothing or equipment well away from such dry things as you have.

A tree pit (Figure 12) is a variation on a snow cave which is possible provided you have snow at least three feet deep and suitable conifer trees. The pit can be dug in flat country and the aim should be to dig in under the lowest branches of the tree. The pit should be no bigger than the spread of the low branches since these form the roof of the shelter. Additional branches may have to be cut to improve the thickness of the roof branches. Any form of canvas or other sheeting could also be used to improve the roof. This is a more basic shelter than the snow cave, but it is quicker to make; an hour should be taken as an average time.

There can be few people who have not heard of igloos and for most people the word brings to mind a picture of fur-clad Eskimos standing in a sunlit Arctic snowscape and carrying harpoons. A romantic idea which is virtually a his-

FIG. 12. A TREE PIT

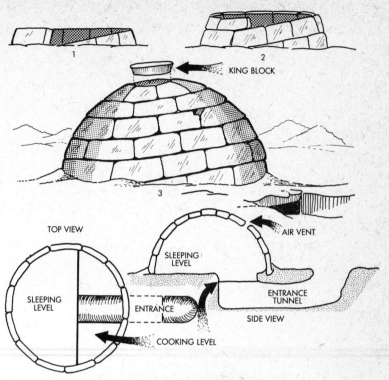

FIG. 13. IGLOO CONSTRUCTION

torical relic only since most of the northern people now live in modern sectional houses in the various settlements in the Arctic. However they retain the skill to build an igloo and will do it in about half an hour. This quick performance is achieved for two reasons; first, polar snow is usually very suitable in its texture and composition for cutting into large blocks with a good snow saw and secondly, the Eskimo has centuries of knowledge of all the nuances of igloo construction. Those of us from more temperate areas do not have this knowledge and only sometimes will the snow be really suitable for cutting into blocks for igloo construction. In a survival situation, unless you have a very good knowledge of snow structure and are very certain, as a result of much practical experience, that you can construct an igloo, my

strong advice is to ignore it and build something else. The fastest igloo I have seen built took three hours and that is just a nice sort of time in which to die in rugged blizzard conditions. However it is sometimes useful to cut some snow blocks to improve the entrance of a snow cave or for some other purpose – at 22,000 feet on Everest we had a rather elegant latrine built of snow blocks – so I add a few words on igloo-building.

An igloo can be built on flat ground or built into a gentle slope. Figure 13 gives the idea of construction which is a gently ascending succession of snow-blocks each of which is canted in. The construction is fragile until you insert the final 'king' block. The outside diameter of the igloo should be about nine or ten feet. This will give you room inside for about four people. The size of each snow block will depend rather on the density and texture of the snow than on predetermined dimensions. Try cutting them about two foot by one foot by nine inches and adjust accordingly. This size may not stay in one piece so cut them smaller. Above this size they will be awkward to handle. The ideal tool is a snow saw but it is possible to cut blocks with other implements although it is far less efficient. Rather than trying to build a long entrance tunnel as in Hollywood cartoons, make a short tunnel and excavate downwards to ensure that your entrance is the lowest point of the construction. This ensures that you retain the maximum warm air. An air vent is required just as it is in the snow cave. Once the igloo has been built loose snow should be used to fill the cracks between the blocks and to make good any defects in your handiwork. The inside should be smoothed to ensure that any melted snow runs to the sides of the igloo rather than dripping on to the occupants. Initially you can obtain some snow blocks from the circular area of the igloo itself, but once you have cut down about a foot you should take the rest of the blocks from a bank of well-consolidated snow.

Any shelter of natural materials will rest upon the ground be this earth or snow. Anything you can do to insulate yourself from the ground should be done. A thick layer of heather or other foliage will increase your chances of survival enormously – and will be a lot more comfortable. You may have something with you like a rucksack, a coil of rope or an aircraft seat that will provide some insulation. If the insulation available is limited, position it under the points where the body exerts pressure – the hips and shoulders. The cold earth extracts heat from your body if there is no insulation and your small body will never heat up the great big earth. Even a pile of newspapers or sitting on this book will provide some sort of insulation.

MAN-MADE SHELTERS

Many parts of the world are not as devoid of human habitation as you might expect. The 1,500 kilometres of the north-east coast of Greenland might seem a pretty inhospitable area, but until recently trappers made a living along that coast catching fox, polar bear, etc., for their pelts. To do this they established a chain of tiny wooden huts complete with built-in bunk, cast iron stove and a few basic utensils. The trapping has ceased but the huts remain albeit in an increasingly poor state of repair. The world is becoming increasingly leisure conscious and as a result holiday cabins can be found in some very remote areas, sometimes only accessible by boat or even helicopter. In Swedish Lapland small sectional wooden huts – *stugas* – have been positioned for the use of walkers as simple overnight stops, thus eliminating the need to carry a tent. Some judicious exploration from your survival site might reveal a very comfortable temporary home. In the United Kingdom the seemingly bleak and barren Scottish Highlands have many now uninhabited farms, shooting-lodges, keepers' cottages, etc., all of which provide a varying degree of comfort but are almost certainly better than lying out in the open for night after night. A ruined farm, thick with sheep droppings will seem a palace after your third night out in pouring rain. 'Bothy' is the general term applied in Scotland to such places.

If a habitation does not offer itself what can you do? You must improvise a tent. Its final form may not resemble the sort of tent you see in a camping shop but it will protect you from wind, precipitation and cold. A tent is basically a sheet, usually of cotton or nylon. Your 'tent' can be a sheet of anything; cotton, nylon, plastic, steel, wood, etc. Two rigid sheets such as corrugated iron can be placed against each other (Figure 14) to form the basic tent. Block in one end with turf and add some more

FIG. 14. A CORRUGATED IRON 'TENT'

FIG. 15. SIMPLE SHEETING TENT

along the ridge to make a rainproof seal and you have a very snug shelter. Those who indulge in outdoor activities normally carry a man-sized bag made of polythene, nylon, Goretex or similar material to use as a survival bag in an emergency. If your sheeting is flexible it will need support. In its simplest form this can be two trees with the sides of the sheet pulled out into the traditional A-shaped tent (Figure 15). Again, it helps to close one end or you will have a wind tunnel rather than a comfortable home. A large log or a small wall can provide a very simple lean-to with the aid of some kind of sheeting (Figure 16)

and this can be improvised very quickly. In well-wooded country where branches are readily available near by, a more sophisticated shelter (Figure 17) can be built quite rapidly. This is similar to Figure 7 except that you are saved the chore of thatching your shelter with natural materials. Flexible sheeting can be made of many things. Cotton and nylon are obvious but also think of rubber sheeting or carpet taken from your wrecked aircraft. Industrial polythene sheeting is used for things like fertilizer bags and carefully cut open these make reasonable cover if several are roughly sewn together (even with

FIG. 16. A WALL SHELTER

FIG. 17. A SHEETING LEAN-TO (WITH REFLECTOR FIRE)

string) or pinned with twig 'staples'. Trees and bushes provide obvious supports, but look for the unusual. On Axel Heiberg Island in the Canadian Arctic I came upon about 40 large oil drums, presumably left by a bush pilot engaged on mineral survey. These would have made excellent supports with any sort of sheeting over them. The only extra would have been a strict 'No Smoking' rule. Your sheeting can be suspended by string or rope or held down by boulders or improvised tent-pegs. Some pipelines use tubes of very large diameter – 24 inches or more – and a comfortable shelter could be made in a spare section of such piping. In the 1950s an expedition to the Antarctic lost part of its base camp hut, but they were able to improvise very well using the large packing case in which their light aircraft arrived. Your comfort will largely depend on your ability to improvise shelter and thus provide warmth.

It is a salutary lesson to watch a well-trained and experienced soldier arrive in a new location, size it up, and set about making himself comfortable. He carries no tent, but has a poncho which he will rig within a few minutes while his cooker is producing hot water for a first brew of tea or coffee. Unless he has other duties to perform he will then get out his sleeping-bag, shake it and pummel it to get the maximum loft from the filling, get into it to minimise body heat loss and then set about cooking a meal or having another brew. At this stage the raw recruit will still be wondering what to do and, if it is raining, getting steadily wetter in the process.

In a survival situation you need to keep your body in the best possible condition. With adequate warmth and shelter you will be able to sleep. A well-rested person can think properly and take the right decisions. There are no rules about when to sleep when in the wild. A few hours in warm sun in a sheltered position are much better as a means of restoring the body than trying to sleep during the cold night. Shivering, believe it or not, is one of the body's mechanisms for generating heat, so never try to stop shivering, it is doing you good.

4. HEY, I'M HERE!:
Signalling methods

You may be six feet six tall and weigh sixteen stones, but compared to the size of the earth you are microscopic, roughly equivalent to a germ floating around in your body system. This gives you some idea of the problem facing would-be rescuers when they start to look for someone who is lost. It is vital that you, the survivor, do everything you can to make your position known to searchers and you must start doing this in the very early stages of your survival planning after you have dealt with casualties and got some form of shelter rigged. Signalling aids range from the most sophisticated radio which can transmit round the world via satellites to you standing in an open space waving your shirt.

AERIAL SEARCH AIDS

If it is likely that a search for you will be made by aircraft, either helicopter or fixed wing, you must devise appropriate signals. If you yourself have escaped from a crashed aircraft, a radio or distress beacon may be available. Approach any wrecked aircraft with care and only when you are reasonably certain that there is no longer a risk of fire. Remember that jet engines work at very high temperatures and will take an hour or two to cool down. If a member of the aircraft crew has survived, obviously he should take the initiative. All aircrew, including cabin staff, have been fully trained in safety procedures and the use of beacons. They will also know the safest way to approach an aircraft. If no aircrew have survived you must use your common sense. A careful inspection of the exterior should reveal wording to indicate where to make an entry. Do not let everyone get in and poke about. If you have someone with

technical knowledge of radios, etc., so much the better. In the survival packs there is usually a beacon which starts to work by pressing a button or turning a switch. Remember that such a beacon will normally work best on high ground, unobstructed by trees, rocks, etc. The aircraft's main radio will be a more complicated affair and may well not have survived the crash, but it is worth your 'technician' having a go. Do remember that military aircraft have additional hazards lurking. They may be armed with bombs or rockets which may have been rendered unsafe by the crash. Also, the crew in combat aircraft sit in ejector seats. If these are not made safe first a rescuer can be badly injured if the seat is activated when he is near it. Usually a locking pin has to be inserted in a hole on top of the seat. This pin is normally fixed to a red label and kept in a pocket near the top of the seat.

Even if you think the beacon is working or you have made the radio work it must be backed up with visual signals. At least one and preferably three fires (see Figure 20) in a triangle should be prepared. Ideally the triangle should have a side of at least 20 metres. The prepared fires must be kept covered to keep the wood as dry as possible. They must be capable of being ignited quickly; if possible, use some petrol to achieve a rapid blaze. Many a survivor has wept with rage and frustration at being unable to get a fire going when an aircraft has been heard. It is vital that someone keep constant watch with ears and eyes for an approaching aircraft. It will pass by in no more than about a minute so speed is vital. Attracting the attention of a search aircraft should not be left to chance. At night the aim must be to produce a fiery blaze. By day your requirement is for smoke; black, if the

FIG. 18. PURPOSE-MADE HELIOGRAPH MIRROR

background is snow or other light-coloured ground, white if it is to be seen against conifers or other dark vegetation or rock. Black smoke can be made by adding oil or rubber to the fire; white by adding green grass or vegetation or small quantities of water. Remember that one of the fires can be your camp/cooking fire which will be going much of the time anyway and it should be easy to take glowing embers to the other two fires when necessary. Keep feeding the fire in case the aircraft has to make a wide turn to come back to check that he has found you.

If you have survived an aircraft crash it is more than likely that you will find in the wreckage, unless it is totally burnt out, some pyrotechnics. These will be either handheld flares, sometimes with smoke at the other end, or cartridges to be fired from a pistol. If you use the cartridges fire them well ahead of the flight path of the aircraft; the pilot will not be amused to have them fired *at* the aircraft and due to the time lag it is unlikely that he would see them.

I was once told by a very experienced pilot that the finest aid to attract the attention of a searching aircraft is flashes of sunlight reflected on a shiny surface. This can be a specially made

heliograph mirror, but the mirror from a compact or a shaving mirror will do. This pilot told me that he had picked up flashes like this long before his aircraft radio had detected the signals put out by a SARBE beacon. If you have no mirror, any shiny surface will do, so find one and clean and polish it ready for sudden use. The method of using the specialized item is shown in Figure 18, but if all you have is something improvised, you must try to ensure that the angle between the sun and the mirror and the mirror and the aircraft is the same. Figure 19 shows this. Remember that these angular equivalents must be the same in the vertical and horizontal planes. Once the pilot has seen you he should waggle his wings from side to side in acknowledgement. If he does this do not go on blinding him with your mirror reflections; he is now concentrating on trying to see you on the ground and he needs unimpaired vision for this. The one limitation to this method is that it needs sunlight, and temperate zones have their share of cloudy days so you must use other signals as well.

Ground signals can be laid out and these require little maintenance. The most obvious is 'S O S' (see Figure 20).

FIG. 19. IMPROVISED HELIOGRAPH MIRROR

FIG. 20. SOS IN SNOW AND SIGNAL FIRES IN A TRIANGLE

This should be in letters as large as possible depending on the available materials. Large boulders, preferably of a contrasting colour, can be used as can strips of brightly-coloured material. The letters can be stamped out in snow, ideally in a north–south line to make the most of shadows. Better still is to fill the trenches you have stamped out with dark contrasting material like tree branches, heather, etc. If you want to convey more than the basic 'S O S' signal, there is an internationally recognized series of signals you can lay out in the same way. Some of the more useful of these are shown in Figure 21. Ideally each symbol should be about 6 metres long, but lack of materials may reduce this. You may have other large or brightly-coloured items such as parachutes, cabin carpets or seats which can be laid out in regular patterns. You must try to make the patterns as unlike nature as possible. Nature is never regular, square, or rectangular.

You may have a torch. If so conserve the batteries and do not use it for reading in bed at night or for illuminating a shelter. Keep it for the possibility of an air search. If an aircraft approaches, keep giving long flashes pointed straight at the sound. Make each flash about five seconds with a two-second interval. If it is not possible to switch the torch on and off easily, keep it on but move it in as wide an arc as possible still keeping it all the time pointing towards the aircraft. If you are with a stranded vehicle remove both the headlamps but leave them electrically connected. When the aircraft is heard turn on the headlamp switch and point both headlamps in its direction. You can produce flashes if someone holds something in front of the headlamps every five seconds. Remember that you must endeavour to make yourself and your position as big and obvious as possible.

GROUND SEARCH AIDS

Aircraft searches can cover a lot of ground in a short time, but they are limited by their availability, the weather and the terrain, so you should always make alternative plans to help a ground rescue party. Remember they may be trying to find you at night or in bad weather and you must do all you can to help. There is an internationally agreed mountain distress signal which is six long blasts on a whistle/flashes on a torch/waves of a garment in one minute, followed by a minute's interval before the signal is repeated. Acknowledgement that the distress signal has been recognized is three long blasts/flashes/waves. Although the signal is designed for mountain use it is equally suitable for any other terrain. If you were to keep making these signals for 24 hours a day you would eventually run out of lung power or your torch batteries would go flat. It is important therefore to decide the best possible time to use the signals.

If you have had an accident, on a rock climb for instance, it is likely that there may be other climbers in the area and the sooner you attract their attention

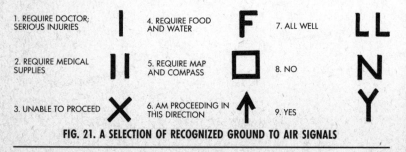

1. REQUIRE DOCTOR; SERIOUS INJURIES	4. REQUIRE FOOD AND WATER	7. ALL WELL	
2. REQUIRE MEDICAL SUPPLIES	5. REQUIRE MAP AND COMPASS	8. NO	
3. UNABLE TO PROCEED	6. AM PROCEEDING IN THIS DIRECTION	9. YES	

FIG. 21. A SELECTION OF RECOGNIZED GROUND TO AIR SIGNALS

the better so immediate use of the signal should be made. If, however, you are in a remote area with little likelihood of anyone else being near no one is going to start worrying about you until you are overdue at your planned destination. It will then take time to initiate a search and for the rescuers to move into your area. Allow the shortest reasonable time for this to happen and then start making signals. Unless you are a large party you are more likely to see the search group before they see you especially if you have sought out a sheltered spot in which to wait. It is vital therefore that one or more of your group be posted as lookouts. You are much less likely to be found if you are carefully tucked away in a collection of boulders well out of the elements, but since you *should* be here for warmth and shelter you *must* have your watchers out.

At night it will be even harder for searchers to find you even if they have a good idea where you are so if you have a climbing rope stretch it out full length across the likely line of approach, thus instead of being a small group only a few feet across you have become a hundred or more feet long – a much easier target to find. Leave the rope out by day; it can still help as can brightly-coloured clothing prominently displayed. You may need your orange anorak for warmth, but someone in your party will be wearing bright underwear and that will be equally eye-catching especially if it is trimmed with lace! The whole secret of signalling to rescuers is to make yourself as big, colourful, noisy and obvious as possible. If you think of the most brash advertisement you have seen on a hoarding or television and try to copy it you are probably on the right track.

5. HELP! I'M LOST!
Survival navigation and movement

In this chapter I have assumed that you have a basic knowledge of map-reading and also of how to use a compass to orientate yourself to the terrain. I have also assumed that this knowledge is with 'proper' maps such as those produced in the United Kingdom by the Ordnance Survey at a scale of 1:50000 for travel over rough country. If the term '1:50000' has already got you puzzled, do read a basic manual on map-reading before you venture much further. 'Being lost' can range from not being quite sure where you are in one of the woods in the New Forest in Hampshire, to being tens, if not hundreds, of miles from civilization in the wilds of Canada. In the first case provided you walk on a constant bearing for no more than half an hour you will come to a road, track or other sign of civilization. You were not really lost – just slightly misplaced. In the second case you have the much bigger problem of deciding whether to stay put and let others find you or whether to try to find your own way out and it is this major problem that I wish to deal with first.

TO STAY OR TO MOVE?

If you are surviving as a result of an aircraft crash in a wild and remote area you stay with the wreckage. It is a large, easily seen object and it should provide some degree of shelter and other useful equipment. The pilot should have filed a flight plan before he took off and may have crashed on or near his planned route. This is the first thing that search aircraft will try. Once you have dealt with the more important of your 'Survival – Immediate Actions' you should send out the fittest pairs in your party on short exploratory trips to see if they can find any sign of civilization. It could

be that there is a forestry logging trail only a mile from where you are. In this case you would be foolish to stay put when by walking even 30 or 40 miles down an easy track you will reach habitations. If you find nothing, you stay put if in the desert or the Arctic. The problems of travel in both these areas cannot be over-estimated. The jungle offers much in the way of aids to comfortable living and local people inhabit many jungle areas. Jungle streams will lead, ultimately, to the coast, but will almost certainly pass centres of habitation on the way.

In temperate zones the decision is more difficult. You should ask yourself if you know your position, even roughly. If you have no idea, staying put is indicated. If you do have some idea of your location, ask yourself if you could navigate to some linear feature such as a coastline, major river, road, etc. The advantage of a linear feature is that your navigation does not have to be too accurate for you to hit it somewhere. Then consider if it is realistic to believe your party, or at least some members of it, could cross the terrain involved and make the distance. Other points to be considered are the prevailing weather, the availability of food and water. A person at rest can last 60 or more days without food, but someone travelling across rough country will last only a fraction of this time without food. Your survival party may contain injured, the very old or the very young. This will influence your decision although there is no real reason why the party should not split with some going for help while others remain. Consider the basic fitness, both mental and physical, of your party. It might be the right decision for a bunch of fit, lean soldiers to try to walk out, but it probably would not be the right decision for elderly, overweight businessmen.

All the above questions are variable factors and must be considered carefully and fully after you have recovered from the initial trauma of being thrown into your survival situation. Twenty-four hours would not be too long to allow for this recovery. If you do decide to travel there are certain things to plan carefully. Those remaining (if any) must be sufficient in number and capability to care for any casualties. Those going must select carefully any equipment they plan to carry with them. They should aim to take the minimum consistent with their own survival. Nothing should be taken 'in case its needed'. They will need to improvise some form of rucksack (see Figure 22) to carry this equipment. Canvas, nylon sheet and straps or rope will provide the basis for such a rucksack. A compass is probably the most vital item and other items are given in the list of survival kit contents at Appendix 2.

The party should pick the easiest route going round difficult terrain rather than fighting their way through it. They

should go at a slow steady pace which is comfortable for the slowest member. Never travel at night, and make camp in time to cook your evening meal in daylight. Always blaze a trail both for those who might follow your route and for yourselves if you have to backtrack. A route always looks very different coming the other way and you should never trust to memory especially if you are getting towards the end of your tether. All the above is in the rather more dramatic type of situation, but what about being lost in the British hills?

ACTION WHEN LOST

Everyone gets lost at some time. I well remember a few years ago being out on the Moelwyns in Snowdonia in thick mist. I was with a friend and we had both recently obtained our Mountain Leadership Certificate as it was then called. He was also a full-time instructor at an outdoor centre. We set off up a path and talked hard about all manner of things until we came to a junction of paths where we both stopped, each obviously expecting the other to take

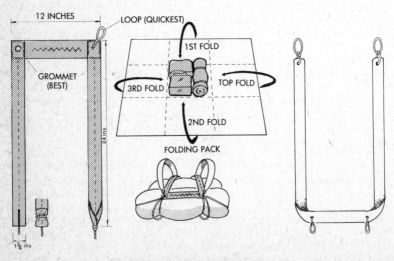

FIG. 22. IMPROVISED RUCKSACK

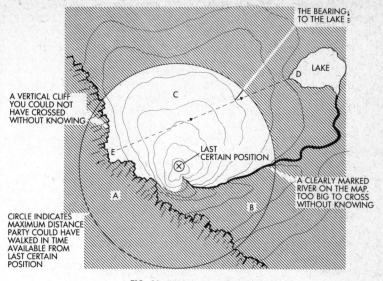

FIG. 23. RELOCATION EXAMPLE

the lead. It then dawned on us that we had both assumed that the other knew where we were. In fact neither of us knew where we were and so, rather shamefacedly, we had to carry out the procedure described below.

The first rule is: Never Get Lost. This may seem to beg the question, but it is a reminder that everyone should frequently check the map against the ground, even in fine weather, and confirm exactly where they are. To do this you must be able to get at your map in five seconds and your compass in ten. That means having them in your pocket not deep in a rucksack. In good weather you have no need of a compass; you orientate the map by natural features, but at the first sign of approaching mist or bad weather you bring your compass into full use and set it to the bearing you want to follow. You are then prepared when the mist suddenly reduces visibility to a few metres only.

If, despite everything, you are lost or even just 'slightly displaced', as an optimist might describe it, *stop* and perhaps sit down. This will discourage

any feeling of panic and the urge to rush on. It will also reassure others who are with you. Think back to the last place where you were quite certain you knew your whereabouts; perhaps a mountain top or a lake clearly marked on the map. (See Figure 23). Then decide, possibly with the help of others in your party, how long ago that was. It is to be hoped that it was only a few minutes; if it is more than 30 minutes I doubt your ability to be in the hills at all. Decide the maximum distance you could have walked in the time that has elapsed. That gives you a circle of distance round your last known location. Beyond that you cannot have gone, so you have narrowed down your present position quite a lot. Now try to reduce it further. Look carefully at your map and see if there are any natural features you could not have crossed without noticing – a vertical cliff is an obvious example! If there is such an obvious feature on your map, you can probably eliminate quite a large slice (Area A, Figure 23) of your circle. Think again about any feature which you might have crossed quite easily, such as boulder-hopping over a stream and which should be marked on the map. This may take another large slice (Area B, Figure 23) out of your circle. Now look at the contours. Have you been going gently or steeply up or down hill? Find the area on the map which corresponds to the ground you have traversed. A break in the mist may give you the chance to get a quick compass bearing on a lake (D, Figure 23) or some other feature in the valley. Are you slick enough with a compass to do this in a few seconds?

A combination of all or some of these actions should be enough to enable you to decide where you are to within a hundred metres or so and Figure 23 demonstrates this process (i.e., you are in area C on line D–E). Having found your position you can then plot a new course either to regain your original planned route or a new route avoiding any hazards shown on the map. If, despite all your efforts, you are still very unsure as to where you are, search your map for a linear feature such as a road or river which can be reached safely from anywhere within your possible area and set a compass course to reach it. This compass course can be fairly rough, e.g., SE or SW, since you are heading for a large feature several kilo-metres long. It might be useful or necessary to climb *up* a little way if this will give you a better view of the lie of the land. For 99 per cent of the time this procedure will bring you back to civilization, but you could be caught out by the other 1 per cent and much of the rest of this book then applies.

In the mountains it has long been a routine practice to leave details of your planned route with some responsible person, e.g., police, a hostel warden, etc., so that in the event of your being benighted, someone will have some idea where you are. A suggested layout of such a Route Card is shown at Figure 24 and on the basis that prevention is better than cure it is commended to all who venture into the wilder areas.

SENDING FOR HELP

The 'Survival – Immediate Actions' at Appendix 1 and listed at the front of this book have been produced as a suitable set of actions applicable to any survival situation anywhere in the world. To that extent they have to be somewhat general in content. Since this book is likely to be used mostly in Great Britain I want to deal specifically with the actions you should take if you have some sort of accident or incident in the

FROM	TO	MAG. BEAR	DIST	HEIGHT GAINED	DESCRIPTION OF GROUND	EST. TIME
OGWEN COTT. 650604	PEN YR OLE WEN 656619	028	1·5 K	676 m	VERY STEEP AND ROCKY	86 MINS.
PEN YR OLE WEN 656619	CARNEDD DAFYDD 663630	038	1·2 K	124 m	BEAR 330 FOR FIRST 200M THEN FOLLOW RIDGE.	27 MINS
CARNEDD DAFYDD 663630						
TOTAL						

FIG. 24. A ROUTE CARD

wilder parts of this country. It is strongly recommended that you take the actions strictly in the order as given.

1. Remove the people from immediate danger. This means getting away from a risk of rockfall, getting the casualty out of the river, etc.

2. Render first aid to any casualties. This is first aid for major injuries not sticking plaster on a slightly cut finger. For the priority of treatment remember C-H-A-S-T-E (Appendix 1).

3. Improvise some shelter. Get casualties into survival bags, build a rock wall to keep off the wind, put on spare clothing, etc.

4. Fix your position accurately. This means a six figure grid reference, and determining any other nearby features.

5. Decide the easiest and quickest route to go for help. This may well not be the shortest. Eight miles down an easy glen is easier and quicker than four miles over a 3,000-foot mountain ridge.

6. Produce a *written* message (possibly on the back of a map) giving the following information:

a. Exact location of accident. Include grid reference and near-by well-known features such as a named lake or foot-path.

b. Time of accident.

c. Casualty(ies) name and suspected injuries.

d. Number of fit persons with the casualty(ies), and whether they have food, sleeping-bags and stoves.

7. Send two people for help. These should be the best navigators provided they are fit. Remind them that the vital thing is to arrive safely at some habitation not that they break all records – and possibly a leg – trying to get there.

8. Dial 999. The two should go to the nearest habitation and find the telephone. They must not go all the way to the nearest mountain rescue post marked on the map. Having contacted the police they then take their orders from them.

9. Those remaining at the site of the accident carry on doing all the things listed in Appendix 1.

DIRECTION FINDING

If you have a compass and good maps of an area you should have little problem knowing where you are and finding your way across country. If you are short of one of these vital items you must improvise. Here are some useful wrinkles. Let me deal with finding north first. If you have a watch which keeps reasonably good time and the sun is out, Figure 25 shows you how to find south and therefore other points of the compass. With a digital watch just draw a watch face with the hands at the time indicated and proceed as if it were a real watch. If you can spare several hours in the middle part of the day, set up a stick as shown in Figure 26 and mark on the ground every fifteen minutes or so the position of the end of the stick's shadow. The shadow will gradually shorten and then begin to lengthen again. The shortest shadow was cast at noon local time and thus the shadow is pointing north. This must be done on level ground. Remember to allow for variations such as British Summer time if it is in force. This is only applicable, because of the tilt of the earth, north of 23.4°N latitude (a line through the middle of the Sahara, the Red Sea, the middle of India, Hong Kong and Miami). From 23.4°N to 23.4°S the shadow can be north or south depending on your position and the date. South from 23.4°S the shadow always points south. This method is good if you are setting up a survival camp but not if you are travelling. You cannot stop for a day every time you want to check your compass direction, but you can make a stop at noon and make a check then to see which direction the shadow is pointing.

At night your best method of finding north is by the stars. In the northern hemisphere the Plough or Great Bear (Figure 27) is the most obvious of the

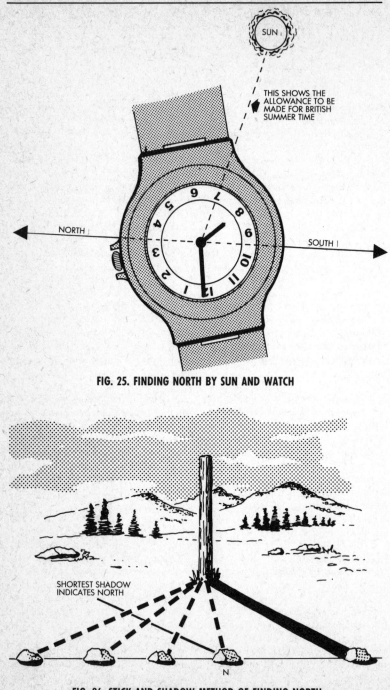

THIS SHOWS THE ALLOWANCE TO BE MADE FOR BRITISH SUMMER TIME

NORTH

SOUTH

FIG. 25. FINDING NORTH BY SUN AND WATCH

SHORTEST SHADOW INDICATES NORTH

N

FIG. 26. STICK AND SHADOW METHOD OF FINDING NORTH

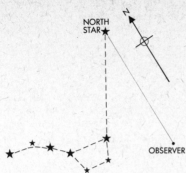

FIG. 27. THE PLOUGH AND NORTH STAR

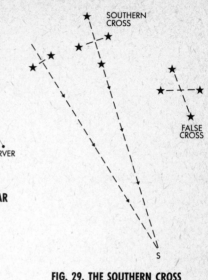

FIG. 29. THE SOUTHERN CROSS

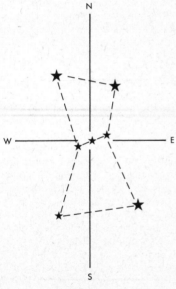

FIG. 28. ORION

In the southern hemisphere the Southern Cross (Figure 29) is the major constellation to look for but beware of the so-called False Cross. Those trained in celestial navigation will be able to apply many more methods of finding north, but the above must suffice for the average layman concerned with survival. It is important to remember that all these constellations revolve so may well appear upside down or sideways when compared to the diagrams given.

There is no scientific proof that humans have an in-built sense of direction. Certain people such as shepherds, trappers, poachers may appear to have this sense, but it is more likely that because of their calling they have become very familiar with every square inch of their territory and thus they give the impression of knowing precisely the right direction to go. Take them out of their own area and they would be as uncertain as the rest of us and this is the reason why a compass or an improvisation of one must always be believed. Some people do have an uncanny

constellations and the North Star, which can be found by projecting a line from the two end stars of the Plough, is always due North for all practical purposes. Another constellation, Orion (Figure 28), is also useful if the Plough is obscured by cloud. Normally Orion is lower down on the horizon and cannot be seen at all in the middle of summer.

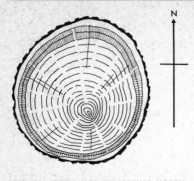

FIG. 30. TREE RINGS INDICATING NORTH

ability to select a good route over rough ground or on a rocky crag but this is not a sense of direction.

There are a number of other alleged methods of finding north. Each has a germ of truth or sense, but it must be stressed that a single example should never be taken as positive proof of direction. If a number of such indications all support one another, the weight of evidence can become very strong and is worth accepting if you are totally without compass or map. In all travel or movement across country remember that everyone is lop-sided to a certain degree and will veer to left or right. In the same way we all have a dominant eye which may or may not coincide with our tendency to veer. To determine your dominant eye keep them both open and hold a finger upright at arms length. Then close each eye in turn. With one eye open your finger will remain lined up on an object, with the other eye your finger will appear to jump to left or right. The open eye which does not jump is your dominant eye. An unbalanced rucksack or carrying a load in one hand will make you veer as will a strong wind or driving rain and snow.

Trees and shrubs often develop in a windswept shape. If you know the prevailing wind for the area you have quite a good indication of direction. Trees normally, provided they are not influenced by rock outcrops, other trees, etc., grow the maximum foliage on the sunny side, i.e., the south side (in the northern hemisphere). If you find a tree which has been felled with a saw the annual rings (Figure 30) will be wider apart on the north side. Moss tends to grow more abundantly on the north side of a tree trunk and the bark on some trees, notably the poplar and alder, is lighter on the south side. In contrast to moss on trees, lichens on rock will be most prolific on south faces. Anthills are usually on the south side of rocks, trees or other objects.

Most seabirds, it is alleged, fly out to sea in the morning to feed and return to the land at night. I doubt that the cormorants which nest four miles inland from where I live know this. They seem to keep up a steady pattern of flying to and fro from the sea to their nests throughout the day so be careful not to place too much emphasis on this type of indication.

It is possible to improvise a rough compass which can be used in conjunction with the sun (if it is shining). First, cut out from card or paper two triangles; one with dimensions 1:2 (see Figure 31) and one cut diagonally from a square. By using one or both triangles in combination you can determine angles as small as 15°, which in survival terms is not too bad. Link this to the fact that the sun revolves around the earth at 15° every hour and you can get bearings accurate to within 15°. Figures 32 and 33 show this in simple form. Figure 32 shows examples of angles which can be achieved by use of the triangles. In Figure 33 an example is given at 1000 hrs, i.e., when the sun is on a bearing of 150° (180° less 2 hrs at 15°). The example shows that the desired bearing for travel is 210° and this is measured with the help of the 60° angle. By 1100 hrs you would have to use the 45° angle and at noon the 30° angle, and so on. A modest knowledge of geometry helps for this method. When cutting out the triangles the dimensions can be anything – inches,

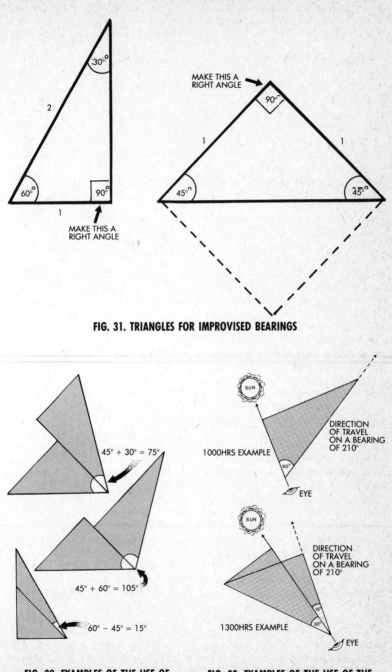

FIG. 31. TRIANGLES FOR IMPROVISED BEARINGS

FIG. 32. EXAMPLES OF THE USE OF TRIANGLES FOR IMPROVISED BEARINGS

FIG. 33. EXAMPLES OF THE USE OF THE TRIANGLES TO FIND A DIRECTION OF TRAVEL

centimetres, thumbnail widths, etc., provided that they are the same on each triangle.

CROSS-COUNTRY TRAVEL

The distances people can travel on foot in a day can vary enormously. On a good road or track with little or no gradient a fit man might make 50 or 60 kilometres in a day. The same man might only cover one or two kilometres in bamboo thicket or mangrove swamp. Before deciding to try to walk out to civilization it is important to assess the type of terrain you will have to cross. Before setting out you should leave details of your intended route at your point of departure and then clearly mark your route with small cairns of stones, a blaze mark on a tree, a sapling broken off in the direction of travel or any other clear indication that someone has passed that way recently. Do not rely on footprints, a rain storm will soon wash them away. Keep a sketch map of your route with the major features, bearings and changes of direction marked in. It is important to be able to measure distance and pacing is the most likely method you will have available. You should know from prior survival training how many normal paces you take per 100 metres. It is easier to count every second pace, i.e., every left or right step rather than every pace.

You will almost certainly encounter streams and rivers. Many books on mountaineering advise against following streams since they have a habit of going over a cliff edge. This is so in some, but by no means all, cases and it is reasonable to assume that you would follow any route carefully and prudently. I see no risk in sensibly following streams and rivers. They lead to low ground and eventually the sea. Civilization tends to be in the lower areas of the world and along the coast. You may be able to build a raft on which to float down a river. This is slow but conserves energy. Do listen and watch for any signs (roaring or a haze of spray) of a waterfall and get in to the side if in any doubt. A raft can be made from logs (Figure 34) or from a sheet of canvas or similar material wrapped round a circular bundle (Figure 35) of twigs and saplings to form a coracle which has been a traditional form of boat on Welsh rivers for centuries. Poles, oars, sails, etc., can be improvised according to your skill and inclination.

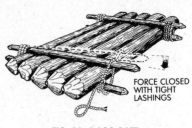

FORCE CLOSED WITH TIGHT LASHINGS

FIG. 34. A LOG RAFT

River crossing is a vital part of any mountain training course, and it is not a subject to be treated lightly. The nearest I have ever come to death was when I was swept away in an Arctic river and battered over boulders in ice-cold water. Remember always to so fix your load that you can easily shed it if you fall over; but having shed it remember also that any rucksack or similar load will act as a float with the aid of which you can half swim half float to the shore. If you can avoid a river crossing do so even if it means quite a detour. If you decide to attempt it look carefully for a good crossing place. You want good entry and exit points. Where a river widens and flattens out it is likely to be shallower. Ideally choose a point where the river is flat and even, and without boulders; shingle and small pebbles are good. It is always worth removing your socks, but put your boots back on to protect your feet. For a short crossing it is probably worth taking your trousers off to keep them

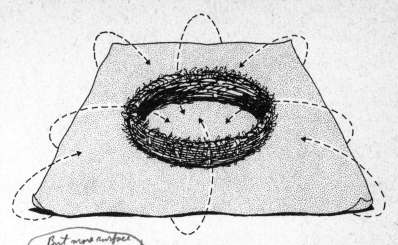

But more surface area for water pressure to hit

FIG. 35. A WELSH CORACLE

dry, but for a long crossing they do provide some insulation against the numbing cold of most river water. If you are on your own look for a stick to provide a 'third leg' (Figure 36), face upstream and progress by a series of sideways shuffles rather than normal steps. If there are two of you, the weakest of the pair stands close behind the other, grips his waist and they move in unison. For greater numbers a similar method applies. A variation for a group

FIG. 36. RIVER CROSSING WITH A 'THIRD LEG'

of three is to stand (Figure 37) in a triangle looking in and with arms around the shoulders of the other two. Again careful control of movement is required. The strongest one should face upstream while the other two face down stream.

If you have an actual or improvised rope the continuous loop system (Figure 39) can be used. The diagram gives one example of how to use it, but additional members of the party can assist by bracing the rope out to give greater support against the force of the river or by providing a downstream recovery loop. If someone falls it is better that he swim/or is pulled to the side rather than try to regain his foothold. In some instances it may be easier to rig a tight rope between two trees, boulders, etc., and each person, except the first and last, ties some sort of loop to the tight rope. Ideally (Figure 38) they should have a safety rope around

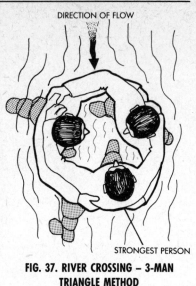

FIG. 37. RIVER CROSSING – 3-MAN TRIANGLE METHOD

the waist so that should they fall they can be hauled in to one side or the

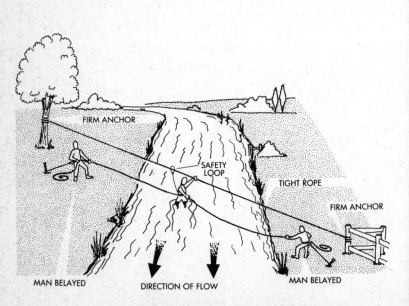

FIG. 38. RIVER CROSSING – TIGHT ROPE SYSTEM

DIRECTION OF FLOW

DIRECTION OF FLOW

FIG. 39. RIVER CROSSING – CONTINUOUS LOOP SYSTEM

other. In all river crossing you should allow yourself to move partially downstream with the current as you progress across the river. Frozen rivers provide an easy means of travel, but you must be sure that the ice will safely bear your weight. Remember that the ice will be thicker on the inside of bends in the river. It is seldom that a sufficient thickness of ice builds up on rivers in Great Britain and all but the smallest lakes are equally suspect.

Ridges and other high land normally provide dryer and easier conditions under foot and also allow you a better view of your route ahead. Against that they are usually colder and more windswept. Remember that contouring can save a lot of energy. Contouring is the art of never losing or gaining height unnecessarily. Climbing up takes much more energy than walking on the level and it is often worth walking further on the level than taking the shortest but steepest route. If you are not sure how two routes compare apply Naismith's Rule and take the quickest route unless you are really exhausted when it will always be better to take the contouring route. Naismith's Rule is three miles per hour of horizontal travel *plus* an extra half hour for every thousand feet climbed. You treat downhill stretches as if flat. Figure 40 gives an example of how the rule works. In metric terms you should calculate this as five kilometres per hour plus one minute for every ten metres climbed.

Scree and boulder fields should be avoided as far as possible, as should any very steep slopes since all these are very tiring to traverse. Snow will add to your

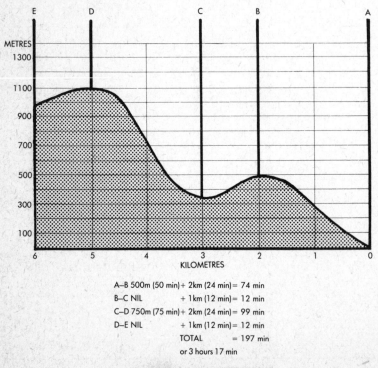

A–B 500m (50 min) + 2km (24 min) = 74 min
B–C NIL   + 1km (12 min) = 12 min
C–D 750m (75 min) + 2km (24 min) = 99 min
D–E NIL   + 1km (12 min) = 12 min
TOTAL   = 197 min
or 3 hours 17 min

FIG. 40. EXAMPLE OF NAISMITH'S RULE

FIG. 41. CORNICE DANGERS

difficulties on any terrain. Soft powder snow without the aid of skis or snow-shoes will sap your energy almost as much as swamp. Hard frozen snow or ice is hazardous without crampons and iceaxe. On a snow-covered ridge keep well back from the edge of a cornice (Figure 41) and note that the fracture line is often much further back than one might think. Avalanche risk is a science in itself, and several complete books have been written on the subject. In simple terms you should keep well away from steep slopes covered in new powder snow, and warm days increase the risk on any slope. Avalanches are not limited to high mountain areas and do frequently occur in Great Britain. Dry glaciers are those with no overlying snow; they are just ice. Because the crevasses are easily seen, travel on a dry glacier is reasonably safe, but even so a rope is a useful aid and only the most

level of such glaciers allow comfortable walking without the help of crampons. Wet glaciers are covered with snow which can bridge quite large crevasses. These snow bridges frequently give way under the weight of a body. It is vital that a party be roped in groups of not less than three. Linear depressions should be treated with suspicion especially if they appear to continue the line of obviously open crevasses. It cannot be stressed too strongly that snow-covered glaciers should only be traversed if all alternative terrain is exceedingly difficult.

Technical mountaineering books explain a number of different methods of crevasse rescue, but the non-mountaineering survivor wants a method (Figure 42) that is simple and easily remembered. The diagram shows how a party should tie on the rope. The principle is that if anyone falls into a crevasse there

FIG. 42. ROPING UP

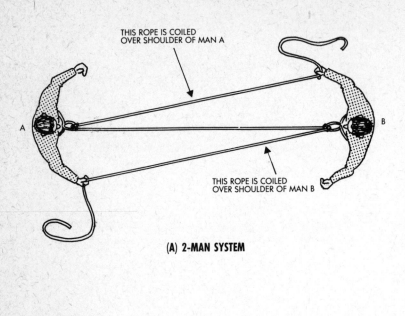

THIS ROPE IS COILED
OVER SHOULDER OF MAN A

THIS ROPE IS COILED
OVER SHOULDER OF MAN B

(A) 2-MAN SYSTEM

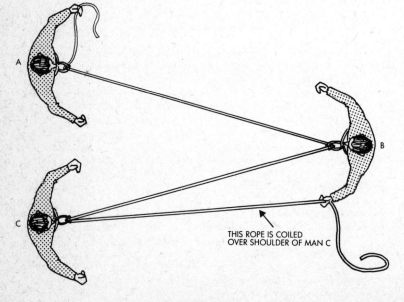

THIS ROPE IS COILED
OVER SHOULDER OF MAN C

(B) 3-MAN SYSTEM

is sufficient rope not under tension to the person in the crevasse for a looped end to be dropped to him. When the loop reaches him he puts a foot into the loop thus relieving the rope pull on the body. It is important that the loop rope runs over something such as a pack, clothing, stick, etc., on the lip of the crevasse otherwise the rope will cut into the snow causing additional friction and difficulty to those trying to pull him up. Unless he is injured the fallen person should do all he can, by pulling on his rope, bracing his feet against the crevasse wall, etc., to assist with the haul. It is possible to reduce the effort required by rigging two-to-one pulley systems, etc., but such systems are seldom retained in the mind unless frequently practised, and this volume is not aimed at the experienced mountaineer who should be well-practised in such arts. Survivors should take heart from the fact that when putting a foot through most snow bridges it is soon sensed and the person is able to throw himself forward or back, or if he does go in he often lodges no more than waist deep, and can be easily pulled out. If you see one of your party fall you should immediately brace yourself and if you have an iceaxe or similar equipment thrust it into the snow or ice. I was once able to hold not only a man but also the weight of a loaded *pulka* (one-man sledge) which hung from his waist when he went into a crevasse. Some instinct had told me he was going through the snow bridge and I turned my skis to take the pull. On my own all I could do was to hold him, but others in the party were able quickly to rig an anchor and we soon had him out. It is better not to carry coils of rope in the hand but to keep the rope tight at all times. On glaciers and where there is an avalanche risk, travel in the early part of the day when it is colder. If you deem it safe, travel at night and sleep during the warmth of the day.

A mountaineering technique which could be useful in a very limited number of situations is abseiling (Figure 43). If you have a rope, double it round some suitable anchor such as a tree, rock, bollard, etc. Do make sure it is free-running because once you have abseiled down you pull one end of the rope to retrieve it for future use. Only abseil if you cannot climb or scramble down easily. You can abseil down a totally sheer face, but before doing so you must be quite certain that you are on the right route and that you will never have a need to climb back up. When abseiling remember it is the downhill hand (the right hand in the diagram) which is the controlling hand. To reduce your speed of descent bring your right arm round towards the front so that the rope is wrapped more around your body thus increasing the friction. To increase speed do the reverse. Keep your legs straight, feet flat on the rock surface and spaced well apart.

FIG. 43. USE OF A ROPE FOR ABSEILING

If, in a survival situation, you have a map and a compass you are indeed lucky, but the map may not be suitable for cross-country travel. It could be an air navigation chart at a scale of 1:1M (16 miles to the inch) – hardly the thing for a party on foot; they might take three days to cover an inch! It might be a panoramic picture map as sold in tourist shops. Very pretty and worthy of a place on your wall but not ideal for accurate navigation. If you decide to move from your survival camp do make sure you understand your map first. Study it. What does it show? Do you really understand how the shape of the ground is indicated? What do all the various symbols on it mean? What is the vertical distance between contour lines? If, for example, contour lines are 500 feet apart a great number of small hills will not be shown on the map. If the contour interval is 1,000 feet things will be a lot worse. Do check the date the map was surveyed. A map is out of date on the day it is printed. Twenty years later it will be even more inaccur-ate with even such apparently long-lasting things as forests swept away. The only features you can rely on are the shape of the ground and water symbols, and even here remember that a valley could have been flooded for a hydro-electric scheme. Remember to check the magnetic variation. In some parts of the world this is massive compared with the five or six degrees current in Great Britain.

No compass is totally accurate and everyone, when they walk, has a tendency to drift to right or to left. Because of this you should never try to navigate directly to a point object such as a single building. In the example (Figure 44) there is a lone hut on the bank of a river, and it is well hidden by forest and so cannot be seen from a distance. If you set a bearing to travel to it, it would be luck or chance if you hit it spot on, especially if you had been on that bearing for several kilometres. You would be to the north or to the south of it. In Figure 44 the traveller has veered off to his left (north of the hut). He

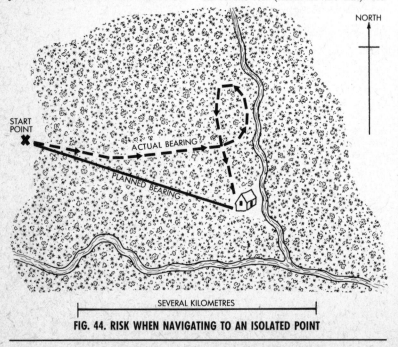

FIG. 44. RISK WHEN NAVIGATING TO AN ISOLATED POINT

thought he was to the south, so he turned north to find his objective. After travelling some distance he realized he was wrong and so had to backtrack finally to find the hut after yet more time and effort had been wasted. The river, being a linear feature, stopped him going too far beyond the hut: it is a linear feature that you must always look for when trying to find a point object. The safe thing to do is deliberately to aim off to left or right by only two or three degrees; then when you reach the linear feature you will know which way to turn to reach the point object.

Navigation may well be a crucial part of your survival in a difficult situation, but it is a subject which needs a lot of experience before you can be said to be proficient. Half a dozen lessons on 'map reading' in a barrack room or a Scout HQ will only give you the very basics and far less than you need to confidently navigate anywhere in any conditions. Even for the simplest of walks on the local common with the dog take a map. See what it shows. Trace out the footpaths. Get a simple Silva-type compass and follow a bearing. See how accurate you are over 1,000 metres. Try orienteering as a sport; you may not win any medals but you will become a very good navigator. For the enthusiast half an hour with a good map will be as enjoyable as half an hour with a good book. If you have not yet reached that level of enjoyment you need more practice.

6. WATER, WATER EVERYWHERE...
Finding water

The shipwrecked sailor's lament continues '. . . Nor any drop to drink'. Fortunately for the survivor in the temperate parts of the world this is seldom the case. However the water that is available will not be coming out of a tap so 'water' must be considered in a survival manual.

At total rest the human body will lose about two pints per day by way of loss through breathing, perspiration and urine. Even if the body is dehydrated there is no appreciable reduction in this quantity. In normal civilized circumstances medical advice recommends that one drink plenty of fluids and the same applies in a survival situation. In the latter case, however, water may not be easily obtained and it is vital to conserve it as much as possible. In Chapter Three I have already mentioned the need to avoid sweating, and the need to conserve the body's store of liquid is another good reason for it. Ideally you need six to eight pints of water per day. As a minimum you need the two pints quoted above, to which must be added a varying quantity according to the amount of work you do during the day. If water is limited there is no value in rationing it to some microscopic quantity per day. There is a real risk you could breathe your last while some water yet remained! Medical advice is that the maximum fluid that can be lost is 20 per cent of body weight.

As an example, with a ten stone person that is 28 pounds or about 23 pints. Assume that the daily water loss is three pints (two pints normal daily loss plus one pint for the additional work of modest survival activity). Without any additional water this will give the survivor seven and two-thirds days. If this person had only a fixed amount of water available, say ten pints, he would survive for an additional three and one-third days (at the three pints per day rate). His total survival time is thus eleven days. To make maximum use of the fluid available in his body at the start of his survival situation he should drink nothing for 24 hours, but thereafter should drink an equal amount on each of his expected day's survival. In this example he has ten remaining days and ten pints of water so the ration will be one pint per day. If he drinks less than this he will die before all his water has been drunk. If he drinks more he will not be eking out his available fluid to the best advantage. Should he find water he can drink unlimited quantities if the supply is unlimited. If it is not, he must recalculate his daily ration figure.

Hot weather or a hot climate will alter dramatically the minimum amount of water required for the body's basic existence. The following table gives the quantity required assuming that the body remains at rest and in the shade.

Mean Temperature °C	Pints per 24-hour day
24	2
27	2½
30	4½
33	6½
35	9

From this table it is quite clear why desert survival without adequate supplies of water is such a shortlived matter. At nine pints per day a person will have lost his 20 per cent of body weight in about two and a half days. The best one can do is to rest in shade during the hottest part of the day and undertake the bare minimum of activity during the cool of the night. A person approaching the 20 per cent fluid loss point may well not be capable of taking rational decisions. For this reason it is probably worthwhile increasing, during the last few days, any daily ration slightly – perhaps by ten or fifteen per cent – to get the fluid into the body before the brain becomes incapable of ordering the action to drink the daily ration.

There is no substitute for fresh water. Urine, blood, petroleum fuels, alcohol all require water if the body is to assimilate them and certain fluids such as petroleum fuels are positively harmful in their own right. Much has been written about drinking sea water especially in relation to survival at sea. However, it now seems clear that since the average proportion of salt in sea water is considerably more than the body can cope with and remain healthy, sea water can only be drunk if there are adequate supplies of fresh water to take up the surplus salt and thus maintain the correct salt balance in the body. Thus it would be much simpler to just drink the available fresh water.

Parts of the Arctic are sometimes described as 'deserts', but this is not unreasonable since the total precipitation per year is often only a few centimetres and is thus comparable to deserts as we usually understand the term. And the term 'desert' can also be applied in relation to the problems that man will have in obtaining water in such areas. Although he may be surrounded by millions of tons of water it will be in a frozen state as snow or ice and every drop for drinking will have to be melted, often by the use of precious fuel in a stove. It is important to remember that the amount of fuel required to change ice into water at freezing point is roughly the same as that required to raise the same amount of water to boiling point for a hot drink. Exactly the same applies in mountaineering at altitude and for this reason climbers and explorers delight to find any source of running water and will

often go to some lengths to use the heat of the sun to melt ice in cooking-pots or spread out on groundsheets, etc. Dehydration is a well-known risk when one is active in cold conditions, and polar and high-altitude rations include a more than average quantity of drinks. The amount of body fluid lost by respiration in cold climates is also greater than in hot and this further compounds the risk of dehydration in such climates. Despite our ability to eat a modest quantity of ice in the form of icecream or ice lollies, eating ice or mouthfuls of snow should never be resorted to in cold climates. The 'fuel' to melt it has got to come from your body heat and in a survival situation you can spare none of that. Eating snow also frequently causes a sore mouth and lips which is painful and unpleasant. Always melt ice in preference to snow. Even a full cooking-pot of snow produces a pitiful amount of water. To avoid burning the pot melt a little snow in the pan first and then gradually add ice to the liquid.

In temperate climates finding water is not normally a great problem, but collecting it and storing it in a survival situation may be. When selecting a possible site for a survival camp one of the factors you must consider is: How far to the nearest water? There may be something of a conflict between proximity of water, of fuel and the need for shelter. You will probably have to improvise water containers from tins, plastic bags, etc. Many good sources of water will only be a trickle. Some Alpine climbers carry a short length of rubber or plastic tubing which acts as a flexible straw and can be used to suck water from the tiniest runnel of water flowing over a rock. You may have to think of something similar and certainly you may have to scoop water, almost literally by the thimbleful, from some trickle source. Some years ago I was climbing in Turkey in an area where the whole climbing programme was governed by the location of two or three waterholes. We first had to find them and from a distance the only indication was the few blades of vegetation – just a tiny splash of green – to show that there was water there. The actual water-hole was only about three feet in diameter and covered with a fair crop of flies and other assorted insects, so the first action was to skim the animal life from the surface and then gently bail out the water with a small mug to avoid disturbing the mud on the bottom. Finding water will often need care and effort.

On another expedition three of us were using a rubber boat with an outboard to travel north in the Inner Fjord area of East Greenland. A sudden squall blew up and we hurriedly made for the nearest land – Ruth Island. We landed and sorted out our wet kit and I went looking for water on an island only about half a mile in diameter. I searched for a long time and was on the point of giving up and accepting that we would have no water that night when I tried one more dried-up water gully and heard the faint sound of trickling water. A bit of digging and removal of boulders and I got down to the water level and used a cup to scoop out the water bit by bit.

Apart from the obvious sources such as rivers, lakes and pools, and by digging in gullies or other water courses, you should always, unless water is plentiful, collect water from groundsheets, plastic sheeting, etc., whenever rain falls. In many streams water only flows in winter or when there has been a lot of recent rain. At other times the watercourse may be dry on the surface but water can often be found by digging down a foot or two. When you find it fashion out a pool to collect the water as it flows in and for sediment to settle out. Green vegetation is often a good indication of the presence of water especially if the vegetation is lush and plentiful. Unlike the jungle where there are plants such as bamboo which actually hold water in liquid form, there are no plants of this type in temperate climates.

Having found your source of water and begun to collect it you have two further problems: to clarify it and to treat it for possible pollution. In the first case, the water may have tiny particles of rock and vegetable matter floating in it. These may be easily visible or they may be tiny. The particles will not give you any dread disease, but they may irritate the walls of the stomach and lead to diarrhoea or vomiting which, apart from being unpleasant, lessen your chances of survival since they remove from the body the very thing – water – which you are trying to get into it. The answer is to allow the water to stand for an hour or two thus allowing the heavier particles to settle in the bottom of the container. Then gently decant the water from the top of the container into another container and discard the possibly murky remnant. Do not be discouraged if, despite this treatment, the water is still peat-coloured especially in an area like the Scottish hills. Just think of it as looking like whisky!

Having removed the large lumps construct a simple filter (see Figure 45) using closely woven fabric. Good quality handkerchiefs are an obvious example or a piece cut from an anorak. If it is a very good-quality anorak made

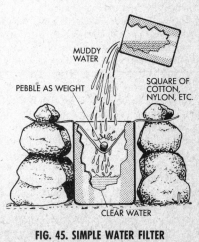

FIG. 45. SIMPLE WATER FILTER

from Ventile or a similar cloth you may find the water only soaks through very slowly, drop by drop, unless you can provide quite a few inches' head of water to increase the pressure. This is the one time when having a high-quality garment is not an advantage. Nylon stockings or tights make another good filter. I must admit that I have drunk water from all sorts of doubtful streams, glacier melt pools, etc., for the past 30 years and have not come to any harm, but I believe that I have a very rugged stomach capable of accepting almost any punishment without a murmur. I have friends for whom the slightest change of food or water seems to mean an automatic dose of Delhi Belly, Montezuma's Revenge, Kathmandu Quickstep or some similar malady according to their geographical location!

Having partially, but at your own peril, dismissed the need to clarify water, the second problem is purification. Doctors will assure you that almost anything except housemaid's knee can be caught from drinking unpurified water and this is certainly true. In the Western world it is possible, with a very high degree of safety, to drink from high mountain streams and I have done this for many years in Wales and Scotland. The proviso is that drinking straight from a stream should only be done above the highest habitation. Water below a farm or house should always be treated as suspect and if you have any doubts use purifying tablets. East of Suez and anywhere else you should always take precautions with the local water even if it comes from a tap. Unlike the British hills where an accurate map will tell you if there is any habitation above you, you can never be sure even quite high in the Himalayas. What appears to be a crystal-clear stream coming down a steep jungle slope from high mountains may be anything but pure. If you follow it up for a few thousand feet you will find some one with his simple house and patch of ground and his pride and joy – a constant flush loo! The only trouble is that his constant flush loo is flushing straight down the hillside into your water bottle. Be warned.

In a survival situation there are three things you can do. First, water-purifying tablets are often found in aircraft survival kits and should form part of your own personal survival kit. They are very light in weight; enough to purify several hundred litres of water weigh less than an ounce, so they should be high on your list of priorities. Without such tablets the next possibility is two or three drops of iodine or a few grains of permanganate of potash in a litre of water left to stand for 30 minutes. Finally, you can boil the water. The pessimists will say that you must boil for at least 20 minutes to ensure you have killed every last bug, but three minutes is usually accepted as a very adequate time especially if fuel is short. Do remember that in most cases water will be boiled automatically to cook food or make drinks. There is no need to boil it, leave it to cool and then boil it again as part of cooking. This will only waste fuel. Running water is usually sweeter to the taste, but is no guarantee of its purity. Conversely, even stagnant water may be pure although it may have a decided taste to it which for the first few days will be deemed unacceptable but will eventually seem like the proverbial nectar. In a survival situation never get so paranoiac about the water supply that you end up dead from thirst but in the best of health in all other respects. It is better to survive alive even if you have suffered a nasty dose of an upset stomach.

If you have any choice in the food you can eat when water is in short supply, limit yourself to carbohydrates – the sweet and sugary things. Both protein and fat need additional water for them to be assimilated into the body. In a survival situation you will succumb for other reasons than a lack of either protein or fats. To sum up, if you have unlimited water drink as much as you like and eat what you like. If you have only a limited amount of water available work out your daily ration and limit yourself, if you have choice, to carbohydrates. Do not worry too much if you cannot clarify water, but beware of drinking it unpurified. Always, for a variety of reasons, avoid sweating and adjust your work rate and clothing to ensure this.

7. FUEL FOR THE FURNACE:
Finding food

Your body is a machine and your digestive system is the boiler or powerhouse. In general if you keep the furnace well stoked with fuel the machine can keep going. In a survival situation your furnace may well have to accept a variety of fuel and fortunately it does compare very well with a multifuel engine. When the going suddenly gets hard, it is not the time to have petty likes and dislikes about food. You may not like rice pudding but if all you have with you is a case of tinned rice pudding you have got to eat it. Tom Bourdillon, who was a member of the successful 1953 Everest expedition, when talking about food once said 'The main thing is that there shall be some' and that just about sums up the hope of anyone who is trying to survive. Vilhjalmur Stefansson, who spent much of the early part of this century exploring the Arctic and often lived off the land entirely, once said '. . . any traveller who complains about going three or four days without food will get scant sympathy from me'. A forthright statement maybe, but it does demonstrate the right approach to the question of food. As I have quoted earlier in this book, food is almost the least of your worries if you are forced to survive in the wild. You will live for weeks without any and you will succumb much more quickly to a lack of water, shelter, etc. However 'any fool can be uncomfortable' and a full stomach will add to your general well-being and help you through some of the other rigours of being a survivor.

If you are thrown into a survival situation you will carry out all your Survival – Immediate Actions and then turn your attention to food. The first thing to do is to determine what food resources you have with you. This may be anything from specially provisioned survival rations in a crashed aircraft, through bars of chocolate, packets of nuts, etc., being carried by individuals, to the remains of a sandwich lunch. Put someone in charge of the food, under your direction, and he can decide what will be eaten, and when. There is much to be said for eating nothing for 24 hours other than perishable items like sandwiches. Even the leanest of us has fat on the body and the sooner the body starts to draw on this the better. Some people appear to have several weeks' reserves scattered around their midriff and similar areas! One idea is that you estimate the probable number of days until rescue and split the available food into thirds. Two-thirds are eaten during the first half of your survival time and the remaining one-third during the second half. Unlike determining a water ration there is no simple way of deciding the amount to be eaten daily other than to say that if the body is kept in a state of food shortage this will ensure that such food as is eaten is digested to the full and every bit of nourishment extracted by the digestive system.

If you decide to send some of your party for help it is only right, since they are likely to be much more active, that they take more than their share of the food. Twice as much should go to the walkers as to those staying behind, provided that the quantity is not so much that they are burdened down by it. As explained in the chapter on *Water* you should, if you have any choice, avoid foods which are mainly protein or fat when water is limited. Most foods are made more palatable and digestible if they are cooked and it also makes them much safer since the cooking process will kill any unwanted bugs. However, cooking does not add food value and in some cases, such as over cooking cabbage, the food value can be much reduced, so do not be afraid of eating food raw if you cannot cook it. To the Eskimo raw liver straight from the still warm body of a seal is gourmet eating beyond measure.

Almost inevitably, unless you are a wildfood enthusiast, you will know very little about the food possibilities in the immediate area so it is important to establish some guidelines on how to decide if a certain berry, fish, etc., is edible. First, avoid all fungi unless you are very experienced in their recognition. In any case 'there's not a calorie in a barrelful', as one American expert has so aptly put it. You will expend more energy bending down to pick the thing than you will get from it. Try unknown foods one at a time. If you try several at once and one (or more?) clearly proves that it is not good for man, how do you know which it is? Prepare an unknown food in the way you plan to eat it. Take no more than a teaspoonful in the mouth and hold it there for a few minutes. If there is no burning, nauseating or bitter taste, swallow it. If within the next eight hours you have no ill effects (nausea, diarrhoea, stomach cramps) eat a handful. If there are still no ill effects the food is safe to eat although for the first few meals it would be wise not to over-indulge. Remember that some foods are inedible when raw, so do not assume that something which passes the test when cooked can be eaten raw. Watch what animals eat. Food eaten by mice, rats, rabbits and similar animals are all safe for you to try.

PLANT FOOD

There are many thousands of plants which will provide you with food; far too many to give you lists of suitable ones. As a general rule avoid those with a milky sap and avoid heads of grain which have a black spur in them. Beyond these two points you must apply the tests given above. While

actual species names are too numerous it is worthwhile reminding you of the different types of plant food. Nuts are probably familiar to everyone if only as one of the traditional items at Christmas. Almonds, hazelnuts and walnuts are well-known and easily recognized and they are widespread in the temperate zones, but other nuts should also be tried. Most of the tiny nuts inside fir cones can be eaten. Beech nuts are also suitable to eat raw. Acorns vary in their suitability. Sweet ones can be eaten raw but bitter ones should be boiled in changes of water, or they can be ground up after being roasted. A type of coffee can be improvised from them in this form. Nuts are a very good source of food as any vegetarian will tell you.

Ferns and bracken, besides providing good insulation or roofing on an improvised shelter, can also provide food. The young, curled-up fronds can be eaten raw or can be cooked if you prefer. Just use the tips since the main leaves will be bitter. We are used to eating wheat as flour in bread, cakes, etc., but all seed-bearing grasses can be eaten. Discard any seed heads with black spurs instead of grain and also any which look as if they have fungus on them. The remainder you should remove from the stalk and then either boil or grind into a coarse flour. The stalk does not make good eating for humans even if it is good for cows. The flour can be used to make any form of bread or bannock. Depending on the sophistication of your survival camp you can make loaves in an improvised oven, or you might wrap a 'sausage' of dough round a peeled green stick to bake a twist over a camp-fire, or cook thin round cakes of dough on a hot surface, such as a sheet of metal. Figure 46 shows a twist being cooked, and Figure 66 an improvised oven design.

Berries and fruits pose problems. Some, such as blackberries and bilberries, are very edible and often form part of a normal civilized diet. At the other extreme are the berries of deadly

FIG. 46. COOKING A TWIST

nightshade and yew which are highly poisonous even in small quantities. However, many more berries and fruits are edible than are dangerous so do not be frightened to try them, but under controlled conditions over successive eight-hour periods. Remember, you can eat the more unusual ones such as rose hips, wild strawberries, elderberries, sloes, rowan berries and many others.

Flowers and their leaves and stalks are another very wide field with many which are edible and a few which are not. The humble dandelion provides tasty young leaves for a salad, a form of coffee if you dry and grind up the roots and the actual flowers can be made into wine. Chickweed, which makes its way into many a garden, can be eaten raw as a salad item or boiled to make a soup. The leaves of the lime, hawthorn and beech are also suitable for salads, as is wood sorrel. The following is a fairly random list of edible plants. Fat Hen, Greater Burdock, Silverweed, all the Vetches, Red Clover, the Plantain group, Yarrow, Goatsbeard, Chicory, Wild Rose, Common Wintercress, Sheep Sorrel; Bulrush (pith of stalk only). Now for the ones to avoid at all costs. Hemlock and Cowbane are both of the carrot family and have leaves somewhat similar to the domestic carrot. Because of this they might be thought suitable to eat but they are not, being poisonous in quite small quantities. Baneberry, Foxglove and all the Hellebores should also be avoided, as should the humble buttercup. Some of these plants have been used in the past for medicinal purposes in strictly controlled doses, but this does not make them suitable for general consumption as food.

At first sight the idea of eating tree bark may seem odd, but the inner bark of poplars, birches and willows is suitable. Scots and Lodgepole Pine bark can also be used provided that you strip away all the outer brown parts and use only the inner white pithy parts. It can be eaten raw but is probably better cooked, either roasted or boiled.

The roots of plants should not be ignored. We regularly eat carrots and parsnips so why not try dandelion, the common reed, and others. Although not strictly roots, the bulbs of onions, tulips and similar plants are all worth trying. Water-lilies and other aquatic plants should not be despised. The world is full of plants and vegetation (including lichens) even in the tundra regions and most of it is good to eat. A book with suitable colour illustrations is the best aid to finding known edible plants and for avoiding the known poisonous ones.

MEAT AS FOOD

Weight for weight meat is the best food you can get, but unlike plants which stay still and allow themselves to be picked, most animals are very wary of other animals and especially of humans. The effort required to find and catch an animal must be measured against the likely food value. Since meat is largely protein, which requires water to digest it, you should avoid meat if water is short. Everyone is familiar with beef, pork, chicken, turkey and other similar meats which form part of our everyday diet, but for the person trying to survive, anything on earth that is animal, bird or insect should be considered. Almost certainly you have eaten a caterpillar in salad or cabbage without realizing it and you may well have eaten all sorts of other things in food. It is the idea of eating such things that we find difficult to accept, and yet in some parts of the world grasshoppers, for instance, are a delicacy.

Since the beginning of time the art of hunting has been slowly perfected by many different communities across the world. Because it is a difficult art, the idea of domesticating certain animals and birds began to be developed a few thousand years ago and now we have reached the point where virtually all meat comes from this source. Only a very few remote and primitive tribes still rely totally on hunting for much of their food although hunting as a sport has become increasingly widespread in the Western world. The survivor has to go back to thinking like his ancestors and thinking 'animal' when it comes to setting snares or deciding where to look for food. Ask yourself where animals (who normally are creatures of habit) would go for water or food. Where are his regular paths? Where would he make his burrow, warren or den? Animals are not unthinking brutes, they like their comfort.

Some years ago I was with an expedition in East Greenland and we were at first puzzled by narrow tracks which looked very like the sheep tracks on the Welsh or Scottish hills. East Greenland, however, has no sheep: but it does have musk ox and these were their regular routes. We then began to realize that they had an unerring instinct in picking the easiest route across country and it soon became the cry of the expedition to 'Follow the musk ox trail!' since that would be the easiest route for us as well. Tracks, droppings, trampled vegetation all indicate the passing of animals. Hole-dwelling animals can be poked out of their burrows but you need to stop up the other exits or have someone there ready to catch them. Hunting at night is possible with the aid of a torch since that will partially blind an animal. Normally animals will be out foraging for food early or late in the day especially if it is hot in the middle of the day.

Before going on to deal with the catching of animals, note that you should avoid some animals or parts of them. You should not eat toads, but you can eat frogs. The internal organs of all animals are best kept for bait, although you can usually eat the heart and liver without ill-effect. The exception is that you should not eat the liver of polar bears or seals, nor should you eat the heads of rats and snakes. Finally, the skin of the snake and hairy caterpillars should not form part of your diet. Beyond these few prohibitions, all creatures which run, fly or slither are good food, but you should try to make sure that the meat is always well-cooked. Some of the meat, while quite suitable as food, may have a flavour which, to put it mildly, is an acquired taste. An example is that the flesh from fish-eating birds such as gulls may have a very 'fishy' taste. However, as the great Arctic explorer, Stefansson, has said '. . . hunger, the best of all sauces, sweetens every sort of food'.

It is convenient to divide the methods of obtaining meat into active and passive. Let me deal with active methods first, although in any survival situation you are likely to try every idea in this book and possibly some ideas of your own; a survival situation wonderfully stimulates the imagination and inventive capability. The active methods are those where you actively seek out and catch your prey, most obviously with a rifle or shotgun. You will be very fortunate, unless you are a soldier, to have such a weapon available, but let us assume that you are lucky. The first thing is to realize the limitations and advantages of the actual weapon. A shotgun, which fires a cloud of tiny pellets over a limited range, is ideal for rabbits, birds and similar-sized animals, but you would be running a grave risk if you fired such a weapon at a bear. Unless you were extremely lucky with your shot you would only antagonize and enrage such a large animal which would then seek out its adversary, and you might well become breakfast for the bear. If you have only a small rifle such as a .22 or a shotgun you would be well advised to stick to small game. If you have the sort of rifle that a soldier might carry in war you can try for larger animals, although you should take care to shoot only if you are sure of a killing. The most vulnerable spot varies between animals, but for a non-hunting enthusiast the most you can expect to remember is that you should aim for the head, neck or just behind the shoulder for the best chance of a kill.

For the novice hunter the best chance of success is to find an obvious location, such as a drinking place or regular track, and to position yourself, hidden as far as possible but with a clear view of your target area. You must note the likely path of the sun since a few hours later you could be trying to shoot into the sun. You must also note the direction of the wind. No animal will approach if your human smell is wafting gently across the water-hole or game trail. Remember that, like the sun, the wind can change direction and you may have to select a new position because of this. Make sure you are com-

fortable, you may be there for many hours. Avoid having any non-animal smells about you. The smell of solid-fuel cookers, paraffin, etc., in your hide, and strongly scented soap, deodorant, tobacco and similar odours will make an animal even more uneasy than your natural unwashed, unadulterated smell. Only clear the minimum of vegetation to allow you a good sight and shot at your quarry. Avoid making any unnatural noise; make sure you have no coins clinking in your pocket, make sure the sling buckle on your weapon does not rattle. Remove all twigs from around your feet to avoid them snapping. Make sure your clothing does not rustle and that the pull on a zip does not flap against the metal of the zip. Only such constant attention to detail will give you any chance of a successful shot.

If you are very familiar with the weapon you will know its characteristics, but if you are not you must spend some time before attempting to hunt anything in finding out how to load it, make it safe by unloading or other means and how accurate it is. You may not be able to adjust the sights, or to 'zero it' in military terms, but you should be able to determine, by firing two or three carefully aimed shots, if it is firing high or low, left or right. Then when you take your shot at an animal you can aim off to allow for any of these variations. Do not waste ammunition, especially if you have only a few rounds, but you must spare two or three cartridges for this or you may well waste all your ammunition anyway. A few years ago I was with an exploring party in north-east Greenland and we had with us three rifles because of the polar bear risk. Only two of us were soldiers so having landed we had a short instructional session and let everyone have a shoot, aiming at a piece of wood with a symbol on it. This was set at the height of a bear approaching and assumed that you waited until it was only about 25 metres away before firing.

Even those who had never fired a rifle before were pleasantly surprised with the accuracy of their shots, although they did express some doubt about whether they would wait until the last 25 metres before firing. Even an absolute novice can be quite an adequate shot if required. A good position, a careful aim and a gentle squeeze of the trigger is all that is required.

If you choose or are forced to stalk your animal your chances of success are much reduced. I have known skilled Eskimo hunters spend fifteen or eighteen hours trying for a caribou without success. However, if you do attempt this form of food gathering keep in mind the following points. Look for any signs of the animals' passing and try to estimate how long ago that was. Move slowly and avoid looking over a ridge or other skyline; look round a boulder, or a clump of vegetation instead. Always stalk into wind and use any available cover. Remain stockstill if the animal lifts its head. Make sure your clothing is dull in colour. Apart from obvious water sources, feeding places and tracks, look along the edge of forests, in sheltered re-entrants, near ponds or lakes. Thick woodland, high mountains and dry areas with poor vegetation are not very fruitful sources of game. Some animals are curious and stand and watch an unusual object such as a man pretending to be an animal on all fours. Closer in a noisy kissing of the back of the hand or imitation of the noise an injured bird or animal might make can also attract their attention and curiosity. If you have already caught your first sheep, goat, deer, etc., use the skin to cover yourself as you stalk.

If you do not have a rifle or similar weapon, try a catapult (Figure 47). It will need to be a powerful one, but rubber ropes (like those used in conjunction with car roof racks) will provide some strong elastic. Small round pebbles will make the best ammunition and you must be ready with a stick or other implement to kill the animal

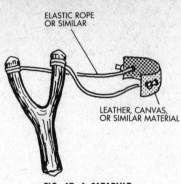

ELASTIC ROPE
OR SIMILAR

LEATHER, CANVAS,
OR SIMILAR MATERIAL

FIG. 47. A CATAPULT

which may only have been stunned by your catapult shot. Even without a catapult a stick or rock may be sufficient to kill one of the slower moving animals such as a sheep especially if, by a combined effort with one or two other people, you can corner it against a rockface or force it over a small cliff. I have never heard of anyone using throwing knives to kill an animal or use a bow and arrow, but I see no reason why such methods should not work.

All birds and their eggs are good to eat, but they have the additional advantage over animals that they can escape in three dimensions (by taking wing) rather than two. Much that applies to hunting animals also applies to birds. If you find their nests the eggs are readily available and many birds especially in remote areas are very tame. At the settlement of Mestersvig in East Greenland I have gently stroked a redthroated diver on its nest without its making any attempt to escape. In the breeding season the young of many species can be easily caught by hand and in the moulting or eclipse season (July–August) many duck are flightless as they grow their new feathers. Birds often nest in colonies and if you are trying to survive near one of these your food problems are at an end even if the diet is a little monotonous! Ptarmigan are usually very tame and can be taken by hand. Some form of net if you have one or can improvise one could help.

Let me now go on to deal with the passive methods of catching your meat. In broad terms these are traps and snares. Indiscriminate setting of these devices will catch little or nothing. You have got to decide the best place for catching your animal or bird; these are generally the same as those for active methods discussed above, but with more emphasis on tracks and regular runs. A simple snare is shown in Figure 48 and consists of a loop of thin wire formed with a slip knot which tightens when the animal runs into it. If wire is not available cord, etc., can be used but the vital feature is that the loop must be held open to allow the animal to get into the snare. For small game such as rabbits the diameter of the loop should be about four to five inches with the bottom only an inch or two off the ground. This type of snare will hold rather than kill the animal or bird.

A refinement of this type of snare is the trigger snare which has the same loop, but the end cord is attached to a branch or twig held in a simple trigger device which is activated by the struggles of the animal, thus lifting it into the air. The device is shown in Figure 49. The trigger can be a stick thrust into the ground, but loose enough to come out when the animal is caught, or it can be a notched stick which is displaced by the

movement. A deadfall can be used to kill both animals and birds. This can be either self-actuating or operated by a hidden man operating a cord. Figure 50 shows the first type and Figure 51 the second. In both cases some form of bait will attract your quarry. Remember that bait is not always of animal origin (internal organs, etc.); for many animals and birds it must be seeds, grain, etc.

I have seen a spring snare (Figure 52) work very effectively to catch small birds in the foothills of the Himalayas. There the materials used are split bamboo canes, but other springy twigs or branches can be used. It is important to conceal the device with grass or other vegetation, and to position it on a likely animal or bird track. Haphazard positioning of traps and snares will achieve little; you must study the animals you

FIG. 48. A SIMPLE SNARE

FIG. 49. A TRIGGER SNARE

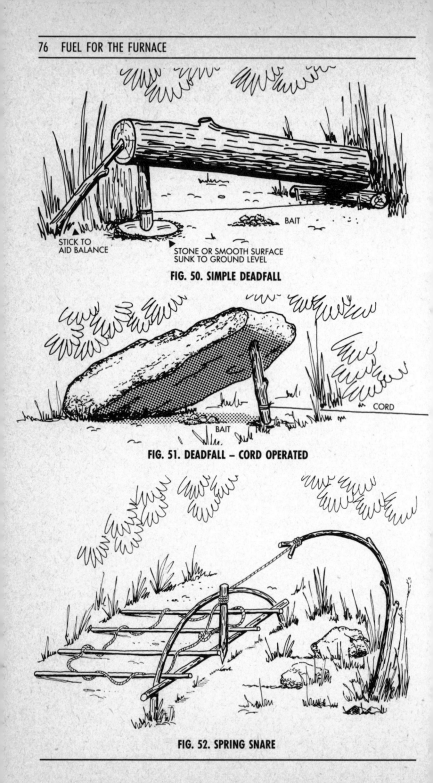

STICK TO
AID BALANCE

BAIT

STONE OR SMOOTH SURFACE
SUNK TO GROUND LEVEL

FIG. 50. SIMPLE DEADFALL

CORD

BAIT

FIG. 51. DEADFALL – CORD OPERATED

FIG. 52. SPRING SNARE

are likely to catch and plan accordingly. As an example, squirrels are tree-living animals and spend very little time on the ground, but if they are plentiful in the area it is worth setting snares on tree branches to catch them. In addition to man-made substances such as rubber elastic, many natural saplings and twigs have a natural elasticity which makes them ideal for spring-type snares. A rather sophisticated one is shown in Figure 53. Unless you have practised making this type before, you will probably need a set of working drawings to use it! Either practise beforehand or carry this book if you ever are likely to need the diagram. Remember that simple ideas are usually the best, but if a party are forced to survive over a long period of time the design and construction of more sophisticated snares, shelters, cooking methods and the like all have a very therapeutic value in maintaining morale.

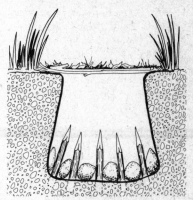

FIG. 53. ANOTHER SPRING SNARE

A deadfall trap is a hole dug on an animal trail or similar place, lightly covered with vegetation to camouflage it. An example is shown in Figure 54. Dimensions will vary according to the animal you expect to catch – and the effort you put into digging the deadfall trap. This is the sort of trap normally used for larger animals and if they are wanted alive. In the past, lions and similar animals have been caught in this way for zoos. The principle can work for smaller animals provided that you remember that most of them are quite good climbers so the sides of the hole must be at least vertical if not overhanging. Remember also that vegetation soon dies off and will require renewal at least once a day.

FIG. 54. DEADFALL TRAP

Gulls can be caught with a gorge hook (Figure 55) which is laid on the beach or wherever gulls congregate, or it can be floated on a piece of wood on the sea. The needle can be made of wood, bone or similar material and must be well disguised with bait; a nice juicy morsel of fish would probably be best. The size of the needle should not

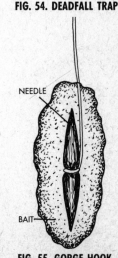

NEEDLE

BAIT

FIG. 55. GORGE HOOK

exceed one inch and the line should be as inconspicuous as possible. Nylon fishing line would be ideal.

FOOD FROM WATER

The sea, rivers, lakes and almost any other area of water will provide food. In the temperate zones of the world the flesh part of fish is good to eat. You should avoid fish with an unpleasant smell, those with flabby skin, slimy gills and sunken eyes. With all fish apply the thumb test by pressing the flesh with your thumb. If the impression remains do not eat that fish (but remember that it could be used for bait). Avoid all jellyfish, those fish with a bony skin instead of scales and those with spikes. Many of the molluscs are good to eat and these include limpets, mussels, cockles, clams, sea-urchins, starfish and many others. Do not eat dead ones; a simple test is that any that are rock huggers will move slightly when touched and cling more tightly to the rock. Crabs, lobsters and crayfish are a delicacy at all times and would be very welcome to any survivor.

Fishing for survival is very different from fishing for sport. There are no conventions about only fishing for trout with a fly or only taking fish over a certain size. You should have a number of fish-catching devices in use all the time, preferably while you are away doing something else. Fishing with hook and line is traditional and you may have someone in your party who is a fisherman anyway. Just as with trying to catch animals it is vital to chose the right place to fish. Indiscriminate fishing will produce little. Normally early morning and late evening are considered the best times, but if you can leave your lines out for 24 hours at a time do so. Pools and the calmer reaches of a river should produce fish especially if there is shade from overhanging vegetation and there are eddies caused by submerged rocks or logs. Like humans, fish seek cool waters in hot weather and shallower easily warmed water in cold conditions.

It is unlikely that you will have proper hooks and line, but these can be improvised (Figure 56) from pieces of hardwood such as hawthorn or blackthorn. Lengths of wire, a sliver from a food tin, unravelling a few yards of wool from a jersey or separating out threads from a piece of nylon cord or rope. A hook and line are almost the easiest of things to improvise. Almost always you will have something suitable for the job. For bait you want as far as possible, to simulate what the fish might eat naturally in the waters you are working in. Remember the trout fisherman ties flies to approximate to the flies that are found on or just above the surface of the water. However it is much more likely that you will have to make do with a fragment of meat from a sandwich or a scrap of sardine from a tin you happened to have in your rucksack. Fish will also be attracted to shiny or brightly-coloured objects, and a tiny piece of silver paper from a cigarette packet or a coloured thread from a garment may do the trick. Do also remember that a worm, grub or beetle may also appear very attractive to the fish you are after. You will need to improvise a float from a piece of wood or cork because you cannot allow yourself the luxury of casting your 'fly' in the best traditions of a good salmon river. You want to set up several lines and leave them to work for you.

Having got your initial fishing set-up going you might move on to more 'commercial' methods. One of these is to build a fish trap (Figure 57). Although the one shown in the diagram has a wide mouth, I have seen traps on the fast flowing rivers in the Himalayas with much narrower mouths and these caught fish just as well. Alternatively you can narrow a stream with boulders, etc., so that the fish are forced into a narrow channel. You can then either stretch an improvised net across the gap or attempt to spear the fish or stun them with boulders as they swim past. A

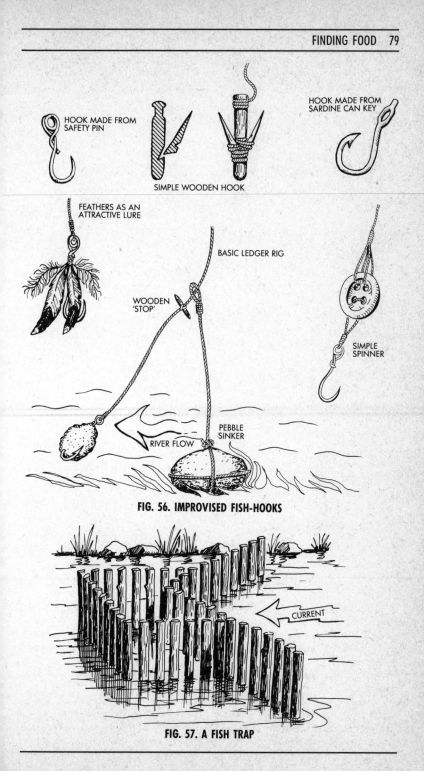

HOOK MADE FROM
SAFETY PIN

SIMPLE WOODEN HOOK

HOOK MADE FROM
SARDINE CAN KEY

FEATHERS AS AN
ATTRACTIVE LURE

BASIC LEDGER RIG

WOODEN
'STOP'

SIMPLE
SPINNER

RIVER FLOW

PEBBLE
SINKER

FIG. 56. IMPROVISED FISH-HOOKS

CURRENT

FIG. 57. A FISH TRAP

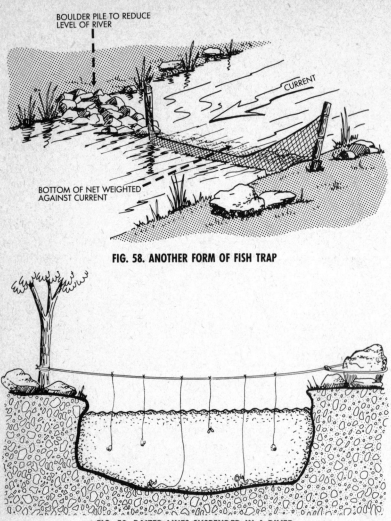

BOULDER PILE TO REDUCE
LEVEL OF RIVER

CURRENT

BOTTOM OF NET WEIGHTED
AGAINST CURRENT

FIG. 58. ANOTHER FORM OF FISH TRAP

FIG. 59. BAITED LINES SUSPENDED IN A RIVER

possible design of net is shown in Figure 58, but you may have to improvise. The mesh should be about one inch unless you know you are dealing with much bigger fish. If you have access to both sides of a river, suspend a rope or cord across the river and attach a number of baited lines (Figure 59) at intervals along the rope.

Do not forget to search tidal pools on the shore or the backwaters of streams.

These often contain small fish which half bury themselves in the sand and can be gathered by hand or some easily improvised hand net.

FOOD PREPARATION

Having acquired your food by fair means or foul, you then have to prepare it and cook it. If you have any fuel available it should be used to cook your food. Cooked food is always safer in a survival situation since any unpleasant parasites should be rendered harmless in the process. The preparation of fruit, plants and vegetables will normally follow the same process as dealing with them in a civilized kitchen. Anything will cook more easily and quickly if it is chopped small rather than being left in large pieces. A modern cook will discard the less attractive outer leaves of a cabbage or the core of an apple. You cannot be so fastidious and you should cook virtually every part of the food, only discarding the really inedible parts which remain after cooking.

The preparation of meat for the pot requires more effort. If the animal is still alive you must kill it. Small animals and birds should be grasped firmly by the head and body. A strong pull with a sharp twist should break the neck quickly and cleanly causing no pain to the animal. Snakes, frogs and similar animals should be hit on the head with a stone or stick. You may be squeamish but by one means or another you must kill your food if you want to eat. An alternative method, and the only one for large animals, is to hold the animal down, pull the head back to expose the throat and cut the jugular vein which lies on each side of the neck. Cutting on the front of the neck merely cuts into the windpipe and will prolong the agony for both the animal and you. Animals should be skinned and gutted as soon as possible. Hang the larger ones up in order that the blood can drain out of the jugular vein. Birds should also be hung up in the same manner. Catch the blood and use it later to add to stews, etc.

To skin the animal place it on its back and cut through the skin on the belly from the anus to the bottom of the breastbone. There is no particular objection if you chose to insert the knife at the base of the breastbone and cut towards the rear of the animal; the

FIG. 60. SKINNING A SMALL ANIMAL

important thing is that you do not stab at the animal. If you do the blade will go deep and rupture the bowel, bladder or various glands which may spoil the meat. You should concentrate on gently using the blade of the knife as if you were a surgeon operating. Having made the full incision, open it as wide as possible, reach in and sever the intestines as high up towards the head as possible. For small animals such as rabbits this can be done with the fingers; for a deer a knife will be required. Remove all the entrails carefully, keeping the kidneys, heart and liver to eat, but remembering that the remainder still have a use as bait. Wipe out the stomach cavity with a damp cloth. Now sever the legs at the first joint if you have a knife or can break them. With larger animals you may not have a heavy enough implement for the job so the answer is to cut through the skin at the joint right round the leg and then cut through the skin along the thigh to join your original cut.

Assuming you have removed the legs at the joint, ease the upper limbs out of the skin and then pull it back inside out towards the head repeating the process with the front legs. If you chose not to use the head for food, keep it for bait. With a large animal you will not be able to pull the whole hide inside out so you must carefully pare the skin away from the flesh. As far as possible you should keep the hide in one large piece rather than hack off small segments. A full skin can be additional insulation between you and the ground. It is often easier to sever the tail at its base before removing the skin. Figure 60 shows the sequence for skinning a small animal.

Having skinned your animal, the next thing is to joint it. The bone joints give you the best guide as to where this should be done, but you may have to resort to some odd shapes in order to fit your cooking-pot.

Snakes, frogs, lizards, birds and all other animals should be skinned and the internal organs discarded or used for bait. If there is any suspicion that the snake is a poisonous type, remove the head and a small margin of the body to avoid the poison sacs. Birds should be plucked preferably while they are still warm as this eases the task, but skinning is usually best in a survival situation. Remove the head and the legs at the first joint. When taking the head off take the neck as well by making the cut close to the body. Follow this with an incision down the back. Ease off the skin as if it were a small mammal. Having done this you should be able carefully to remove all the intestines. As when skinning animals, you must avoid rupturing the gall bladder, bowel, etc.

Fish are easy to gut. Remove the tail and the head at the gills. Lay the fish on its side on a flat surface and with as sharp a knife as possible cut on the underside of the fish from the tail end to the head. Remove the internal organs and wash the whole fish, preferably in running water. A professional fishmonger with his array of knives will fillet a fish with ease, but in a survival situation it is probably best not to attempt this, but to cook the fish whole or at least in large cutlets, then removing the meat from the bone when cooked.

COOKING METHODS

You may be fortunate in your survival situation and have some form of cooking-stove. This may run on paraffin, petrol, meths, camping gas or solid fuel. This is the ideal, but there are two limitations. First, you must know how to use the stove safely. Correctly operated, all stoves are safe but they all depend on using a very flammable fuel which will cause bad burns if misused. Any survival situation produces problems; do not compound them by having a badly burned person in your party as well. Secondly, you will almost certainly have a finite amount of fuel. In an extreme case you might be with an aircraft which has crash-landed successfully with a tankful of aviation turbine fuel intact. This could be thousands of litres and would keep the average primus type paraffin stove going for months even if you burned it 24 hours a day. Whatever fuel you have, conserve it to the utmost.

Recently on an expedition to Greenland I cooked for ten days with one litre of meths. I had reasonable meals and did not stint myself on brews of coffee, but I never let the stove burn for an instant without something on it even if it was just a tiny drop of water for washing up. You must never 'waste' fuel for space heating. Your bodily warmth must come from clothing, sleeping-bag or other insulation. Eventually your fuel will run out and you are then back to natural materials.

Before dealing with types of fires and improvised cooking methods a word or two on means of ignition might help. All the fuel in the world is just so much useless rubbish if you cannot set light to it. Matches and cigarette lighters are the most obvious forms of ignition but should be used in conjunction with a candle if you have one. They could well be the means of saving your life, and you cannot take too much care of them. Always carry matches in an inner pocket, wrapped and sealed in a polythene bag and where the warmth of your body can help to keep them dry. Never be content to carry just one box or book of matches; their weight is negligible so always have one or more spares in your clothing or kit. It is well worth carrying some in a waterproof container and you might consider having an emergency reserve either of ordinary matches which you have previously waterproofed by covering in candle wax, or of what are known as lifeboat matches. These will burn fiercely in almost any conditions of rain, wind, etc. A cigarette lighter is another way of causing fire and this should be carefully nurtured in some warm dry place about your person rather than left to get at least damp if not wringing wet in an unprotected outside pocket.

Non-smokers should remember to carry matches or a lighter in case they are ever in a survival situation. It is perhaps the only advantage in being a smoker that you will automatically have a means of fire with you. Treat every match and every flick on the lighter as if it were your last one. You may have to ration matches just as you ration food and it should be a firm rule that you never, no matter how bad the situation, light a match until the fuel and everything else is ready and you have taken every precaution against wind, rain and any other natural hazards. Only then do you light your stub of candle and use that to light your fire or stove. Once that is alight, extinguish your candle and keep it for next time.

If you have not got matches or a lighter what can you do? Provided the sun is shining, a lens removed from a pair of binoculars or a camera will do the trick. Focus the rays of the sun through the lens to a pinpoint on the tinder and it should soon start to smoulder and eventually burst into flames. On the commercial market are a number of gadgets which will produce a spark. Most of them depend on the phenomenon that striking steel against flint or similar substance will produce a spark. If you are devising your own survival kit you might choose to include one of these things instead of or in addition to matches. They have the advantage that they will usually produce more sparks than a single box of matches, but your tinder (which is

FIG. 61. FLINT, STEEL AND MAGNESIUM FIREMAKING

no! use back - not edge
of knife

sometimes also provided by means of a magnesium block) must be even better at igniting than tinder used with matches (see Figure 61). If you have a powerful battery from a car or aeroplane, this will produce excellent sparks by shorting across the terminals. Flints sometimes occur naturally especially in parts of the country where the basic rock is chalk. They will be single, hard and usually misshapen rocks embedded in the chalk. Dig one out, split it open and you will have a readymade flint.

Some native tribes can make fire by rubbing two sticks or other pieces of wood together. These tribes are almost exclusively found in places where tinder-dry wood is readily available. In temperate zones this is very unlikely and even the aforementioned tribes, having kindled their fire, will often carry it with them when they move on rather than go to the trouble of relighting it. You are more likely to have success with a firebow (see Figure 62). The stick should be a hardwood (from a deciduous tree) with a sharpened point at one end. The board is softwood (from a coniferous tree) with a depression cut out of it to take the pointed end of the stick. Make the bow from a flexible branch and use string, shoelace, or something similar for the string of the bow. Nylon cord is not very good for this because it does not grip the stick well enough to turn it. Press down on the top of the stick with a flat rock or similar pad and move the bow backwards and forwards to rotate the stick rapidly. Some of your tinder should be in the depression. This is the theory and I know people who have succeeded, but I must confess that I have not done so myself. It certainly needs a lot of effort!

Having got your means of ignition you need tinder. The vital requirement is that it be bone dry. We use the term 'tinder-dry' in everyday speech to indicate something which is extremely dry. Leaves, the bark from birches and hawthorns, wool from sheep or your jersey, virtually any bits of fluff, feather or down, scraps of lint, cotton wool, materials, tiny wood shavings taken from the inner wood of a tree branch of a pine, grass and other similar-sized

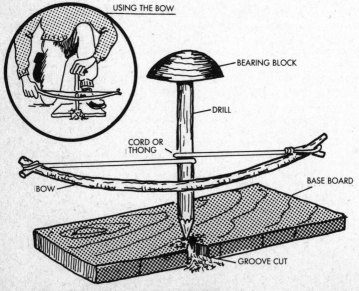

USING THE BOW

BEARING BLOCK

DRILL

CORD OR THONG

BOW

BASE BOARD

GROOVE CUT

FIG. 62. A FIREBOW

pieces of vegetation are all possible sources for tinder. If you are fortunate enough to have some petrol, meths or similar fuel, a few drops – and no more – will make lighting the tinder much easier. Quite apart from the danger of a sudden flareup if you use too much petrol, remember you conserve everything and anything when you are a survivor and even something as insignificant as a little bit of fuel could be the difference between life and death.

Before lighting your tinder, however, make sure you have twice as much heavier fuel ready as you think you will need. There is nothing worse than getting a fire going nicely and then seeing it die because you have not gathered sufficient fuel to keep it going. If you can, choose the type of wood for the fire you need. For getting a fire going use birch or almost any coniferous tree. Once the fire is going and if you want a good cooking-fire (or warming-fire) to last a long time, change to oak, ash or beech. Poor woods for any sort of fire are elm, chestnut, willow and poplar. If you can pick and choose you will be very lucky indeed. It is much more likely that you will be burning heather roots, ground willow and other not very satisfactory fuels. Remember that dried dung, peat and animal fat can also be used as fuel.

Having gathered your fuel you are at last ready to start your fire. Choose a

CUT HERE

why?

FIG. 63. A FUZZ-STICK

sheltered spot on dry ground. An overhanging rock could shelter you and your fire from rain and snow. If there is snow on the ground build a platform of green logs and build your fire on that. It can be useful to have a fuzz-stick (see Figure 63) as the centre post of your fire to help start it. Put your other tinder round it and then some slightly thicker twigs (no thicker than a quarter of an inch) in a pyramid shape. Leave a small opening for your match to be applied. Figure 64 shows what it should look like. Shelter the fire from the wind with your body and cup the matchbox in your hands. Light the match carefully and get it well alight before applying it

TINDER

KINDLING

FIG. 64. HOW TO START A FIRE

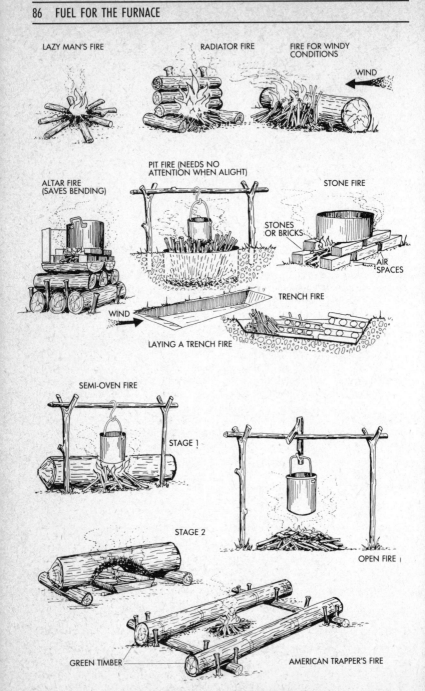

LAZY MAN'S FIRE

RADIATOR FIRE

FIRE FOR WINDY CONDITIONS

WIND

ALTAR FIRE (SAVES BENDING)

PIT FIRE (NEEDS NO ATTENTION WHEN ALIGHT)

STONE FIRE

STONES OR BRICKS

AIR SPACES

WIND

TRENCH FIRE

LAYING A TRENCH FIRE

SEMI-OVEN FIRE

STAGE 1

STAGE 2

OPEN FIRE

GREEN TIMBER

AMERICAN TRAPPER'S FIRE

FIG. 65. A SELECTION OF DIFFERENT TYPES OF FIRE

to the fire. Add fuel gently so that you do not stifle the fire. In the early stages you want dry wood so you may have to split the timber open to get at the centre wood. Gradually build up the fire until it is the size you want. This will normally be the smallest possible for cooking your food. Large fires are no better for cooking and are difficult to get near, but more importantly you will waste energy gathering timber to keep such a fire going and a survivor must conserve everything – not least his own energy. If you want a fire to sit round or to dry clothing, still make it a small one but sit close to it. Camping books usually show a number of neatly drawn diagrams of different types of fires. Figure 65 gives some examples, but do not try to follow these slavishly, your facilities or surroundings may not be right. Remember that a good bed of ashes is best for cooking rather than a mass of flames which the cook cannot get near.

It may seem odd to talk about improvising an oven in a survival situation but it can be useful and the devising of it can interest several people for some time – a good fillip to morale in difficult circumstances. A five-gallon oildrum or similar container is the sort of thing you need. Figure 66 gives an idea of the possibilities. The 'fire' could be a cooking-stove or a wood fire. Ideally it should be dug into an earth bank but this is not vital. There must be a through draught to keep the fire going and you need some form of sheet as the door. Some years ago on an expedition to the Canadian Arctic one of the party found an old oildrum in the middle of the tundra and improvised an oven. We had some breadmix with us and he produced some very acceptable loaves.

We have dealt so far with what is basically a camp-fire even though it can be made in many different forms and with all sorts of variations; but what other methods of cooking are there? If you have an easily ignited fuel such as petrol you can make what was known during the Second World War as a

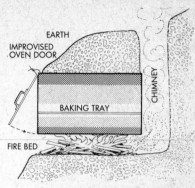

FIG. 66. IMPROVISED OVEN (SECTIONAL VIEW)

FIG. 67. A BENGHAZI BURNER

Benghazi Burner. Put an inch or two of sand or similar soil in the bottom of a tin. Punch, bore or cut holes just above the sand to provide a source of oxygen for the fire. At the top of the tin (see Figure 67) cut some slots to allow the smoke to escape. Depending on what is available and the amount of fuel this could be done with a very small food tin or a large Army biscuit tin. A variation of this uses a candle instead of petrol and sand. Obviously this can only be done with a very small food tin, but because the heat is contained within the tin very little is lost to the surrounding atmosphere and a flame as small as a candle will heat water for tea, soup or coffee. If you have the ingredients you

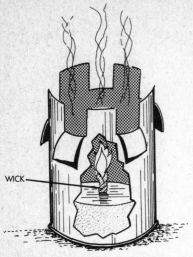

FIG. 68. IMPROVISED STOVE FOR OIL, FAT, ETC.

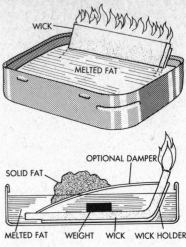

FIG. 69. ANOTHER TYPE OF IMPROVISED STOVE

can even make tiny drop scones on a small piece of metal placed across the top. A similar principle of heat conservation is used by the makers of the Trangia type of cookset.

For centuries the Eskimos have used seal blubber as a source of heat and light, but for this and when using any of the less combustible oils you need a wick, so if you have engine oil, animal fat or even some insect repellant make yourself a stove or 'koodlik' as it is called by the Eskimos. For a wick you can use string, a strip of rag, nylon cord or even dried moss. Figure 68 shows a stove using an upright tin and Figure 69 a shallow tobacco-type tin. Do be careful when lighting the more volatile fuels, and if you want to make a petrol stove last longer add a little oil or similar less explosive fuel.

These designs for improvised stoves are also useful if you are very restricted for fuel – perhaps nothing more than a few heather roots. Substitute these for the candle and keep the tiny fire going carefully and you will again be able to heat water for a hot drink even if you cannot cook a meal.

Cooking is an art. One person will, from a few odds and ends, produce a meal fit for a king. With the same odds and ends someone else will produce an almost inedible mess, except for the fact that for survival nothing is inedible – all must be eaten. As far as possible maintain your standards and try to produce meals as close as you can to those you might eat in civilized circumstances. Beware the man who wants to throw everything into one pot. You may only have one pot but try to do better than that. Such a meal will always be a tasteless mess. The best way of cooking food in a survival situation is by boiling. Almost all food can be boiled and it loses little of its food value in the process provided that you keep the cooking water and consume that as well in the form of soup or mixed with other foods. For the pedantically minded cook the term boiling should be taken to include stewing. It is the safest form of cooking to ensure that parasites in meat are killed, vegetables are softened and allows even the most unlikely food such as lichens to be added. You may be lucky enough to find some wild

FIG. 70. SPIT ROASTING

herbs to add to your stew and make it more appetising. Your boiling-container may have to be improvised so do not be too rigid in thinking solely of the saucepans you would find in a proper kitchen. You can boil water in a paper-bag with care. the air-sickness bags provided in aircraft are very good for this.

If you have no means of boiling you will have to resort to roasting. Almost any small animal or fish can be cooked (see Figure 70) on a spit over a good bed of embers. For a quicker meal cut the meat and vegetables up and skewer the

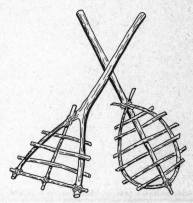

FIG. 71. GRIDDLES

FIG. 72. COOKING ON A STRING

pieces on a suitable piece of metal or a peeled green stick. The result is kebabs – a very popular barbecue dish. Avoid sticks from yew, laurel and pine which will taint the food. Griddles improvised from thin saplings or branches (see Figure 71) can also be used to roast meat. If you have the ingredients to make any form of bread, roll out the dough into a long 'sausage' and wrap it round a green stick (see Figure 46) to bake in the heat of the fire. This is known as a twist. Dough can be shaped into a round disc and baked on any flat surface over the fire. You could suspend a succulent bird's leg from a string (Figure 72). Before cooking any meat by roasting thrust it into a flame for a few seconds to seal the outside surface.

If you are going to bake your food in the embers of your fire, only gut your animal, bird or fish; leave the skin, scales or feathers on. Wrap the whole thing in clay, mud or large, wet leaves and scrape away the embers of a fire which has been going for some time so that the ground underneath is well heated. Place your food pack in the embers and rake them over it. A rabbit-sized animal will take at least an hour. This is a traditional gypsy method of cooking hedgehogs. When the meal is cooked break open the clay and you will find that most of the fur, feathers, etc. (or spines in the case of a hedge-hog!), will come away with the clay, leaving the meat or fish ready to eat. If you wish you can use the same method (with leaves only) for a piece of meat and include some vegetables with it. Aluminium foil, which is often used in aircraft for various technical parts, can be used instead of the leaves. The gourmet touches can be provided by including some herbs with the food. Instead of just scraping away the embers of your fire you can dig an oven hole (Figure 73). Heat some stones in your fire and then place them in the bottom of the hole. Some types of stones have a tendency to split when heated, and these should be discarded. Let the stones start to warm the hole and then put in some embers, followed by your food and some more embers. Add some new fuel to the top layer of embers and keep it going like any other fire. You can cook something else on this top fire. Cooking times will vary according to the size of your meat, fish, etc., but 40 minutes would be a good start. Trial and error will show how to adjust this time. If you want to cook something slowly, perhaps while you

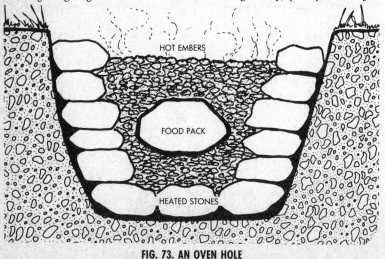

FIG. 73. AN OVEN HOLE

are away from your survival camp, omit building the fire on top and just put some turf over the hole. Smaller items of food such as eggs, shellfish or snails can be cooked in this sort of pit. Wrap them in leaves, grass or cloth, cover with half an inch of sand or soil and build a fire on top.

Frying food should be your last resort, but if you have a plain sheet of tin which you cannot fashion into a better cooking-pot, then by all means fry your food. A hot flat stone can also be used for frying but you must maintain its heat. All food is best cooked as soon as possible after you have obtained it. If you have a ready source of food only gather what you need as you require it. However, this is very much an ideal and most of the time you will be only too glad to get any food that is available when it is available. Previously prepared rations are dealt with on page 120.

I started this chapter by saying that food was not your most pressing problem in a survival situation and that you could live for several weeks without it. While this is quite true, nevertheless, within a few days the lack of food will begin to take its toll of your physical and mental capabilities, and this in turn will reduce your chances of ultimate survival. For this reason you should make every effort to find, prepare and consume food of all sorts. The morale of a party will sink to a very low level if they do not eat. Determination will dwindle and apathy will ensue. This is the road to failure and death. Find food and eat it!

8. A HEALTHY MIND IN A HEALTHY BODY: Survival medicine

You stand a better chance of survival if you are mentally and physically fit. This is one good reason why in everyday life you should keep yourself in this desirable state, because a survival situation is hardly the time to start a regime to improve your fitness. However, even the fittest person can be injured or be taken ill. The very action of your being precipitated suddenly into a survival state may have caused injury to you or one of your companions, but even if this is not the case initially, something may happen before you are rescued and you will be faced with a medical problem of some sort. Just as with every other aspect of survival, training and practice before the event is of great value, so it is with the medical aspect, but here there is a much greater chance of your training and skills being used. Only a small proportion of the population will, within their lifetime, be likely to find themselves fighting for survival. For those who work or take their leisure in the outdoors the proportion will, of course, be higher. Few, if any, of us will go through life, however, without needing some knowledge of first aid or minor medicine. We will arrive on the scene of a road accident, our child will be badly cut by broken glass on the beach, a husband will electrocute himself doing a household repair or a wife will burn herself badly on the kitchen stove. One or more of these incidents will come our way during our 70 or so years on this earth.

In the Survival – Immediate Actions (see Appendix 1) I have given a mnemonic – C-H-A-S-T-E – as a help to you when suddenly presented with an accident. Even if you have done a course of training with one of the national first aid organizations, when you approach your first accident all that you have learned will seem to disappear from your brain just when you need it. Remember CHASTE and what it means and you will do things in the right order. Let me deal with each part in turn.

C – CHOKING, CARDIAC

With any casualty the vital thing is to get him breathing again if he has stopped. Clear his mouth and throat of any obstruction and then begin one of the methods given in first-aid manuals. The generally recommended method is popularly called the 'kiss of life'. Get the casualty into the position shown in Figure 74 as quickly as possible, give four quick full breaths with your mouth sealed over the casualty's and with his nose pinched shut between your fingers and thumb. When you have done this settle down to a breathing rate of about twelve to fifteen cycles per minute, i.e., you breathe into his mouth then take your mouth away to allow him to exhale. As well as not breathing the casualty's heart may have stopped. Check this by feeling his pulse at the wrist with your fingers. If you cannot detect it you should endeavour to get his heart going again. Figure 75 gives you the method of doing this. Remember that the heartbeat is much faster than the lung rate so your pressure applied at the base of the breastbone should be about 70 per minute. Do not muddle this with the twelve to fifteen breaths per minute to get the breathing going! This is just a brief summary of the methods in common use (and there are other methods you can use if, for instance, your casualty has a badly damaged face or mouth), but you cannot learn to do these procedures correctly from a book. Take a proper

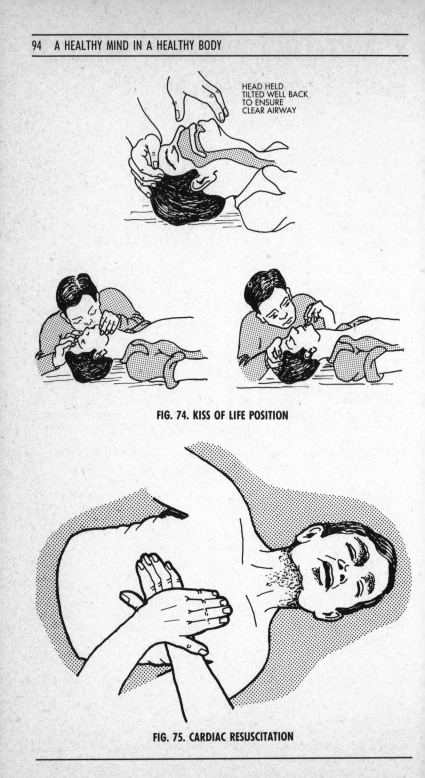

FIG. 74. KISS OF LIFE POSITION

FIG. 75. CARDIAC RESUSCITATION

course or at least get someone who is already trained to show you what to do. Remember that if the pulse has stopped and the lungs are not functioning irreversible damage will soon occur to the brain and other parts of the body so you must have a go. Even if you are not sure of every detail, you will seldom have time to wait for more skilled help to arrive. You may get it wrong, but you are much more likely to get it right and save a life.

H – HAEMORRHAGE

The next most likely cause of early death is heavy bleeding. Having got your casualty breathing and his heart going you must do a rapid body check to see if he is bleeding badly; not a badly grazed hand or even a deeply cut finger, but major bleeding, probably from an artery or vein where the blood is literally pouring out, and already soaking into the clothing. The first treatment is to apply pressure to the wound with a pad of some sort. Check quickly that there is no piece of jagged glass in the wound, but do not worry about getting out all the tiny bits of dirt that may be there, nor should you worry about having a clean, sterile dressing to apply. This is nice if you have it, but it is better for the casualty to be alive even with a few extra bugs floating round his system (which modern antibiotics will deal with) than dead while waiting for a clean dressing to arrive. If you have no cloth pad of any sort your fingers will provide a very good means of closing a wound, and blood, even lots of it, is just a red, slightly sticky liquid which can do you no harm whatsoever. If the blood begins to soak through the first pad apply another, tying it firmly over the first. If possible, and other injuries allow, elevate the wound above the level of the heart. With bad bleeding you may also apply pressure at one of the pressure-points situated in various parts of the body. Tourniquets should only be applied by trained medical staff

except in the case of total severence of a part of a leg or an arm.

A – ASSISTANCE

Having dealt with the real killers of Choking, Cardiac Arrest and Haemorrhage, you can now take a very short breather and consider getting some Assistance. At a normal road accident this would mean sending someone to find the nearest telephone and to call an ambulance. In a mountain accident a mile or two from a road, you would send off two of your party to contact the police. The assistance would, in due course, arrive and this sort of thing is now a routine affair in most civilized countries. However, if you are miles from anywhere, or in an area with no sophisticated facilities, you have got to do a lot more for yourself. Your Assistance must come from those with you and you must appoint someone to look after the casualties while you get on with the bigger problem of the survival of the whole party rather than just those who are injured.

S – SHOCK

Shock will occur with every injury no matter how small, even if there has been no physical injury but only an emotional one such as being involved in a car crash. The shock from a cut finger is so slight that we normally take no notice of it and carry on with whatever we are doing, but the shock from a major injury, if left untreated, can be a contributory cause of death. The treatment is simple. Warmth, comfort and reassurance are required, and a hot drink provided that the casualty has no internal injuries. After something as traumatic as an air crash everyone including yourself will have some degree of shock and you should remember this. The will to carry out life-saving procedures must be summoned up, but thereafter a time of rest and recovery should be allowed for everyone. A quickly organized camp and then time set aside for sleep will deal with shock.

T – TREATMENT

Having made your casualties warm and comfortable you can now deal with their other injuries. Speed is no longer the priority so you can attend to them with more care and consideration. If the casualty is conscious start at his head and work gently down the body asking him where, if at all, he has any pain. Some injuries such as a bad burn will probably be obvious, but others, such as a simple fracture may not be obvious especially if concealed under clothing. A conscious patient will naturally adopt the least painful position. It is normally best to leave him in this position but to provide support, e.g., with splints for a broken arm, or a sling to support the arm if the collarbone is broken.

If the casualty is unconscious carry out the body check and take any precautions you think fit to avoid an injury being made worse. An open fracture where the broken end of the bone has pierced the skin should obviously have a dressing placed over the wound. Any burn should be covered with a dressing to exclude the air and thus reduce the pain. No attempt should be made to give food or drink to an unconscious patient nor do they need pain-killers of any sort; their natural body mechanism has done the job for you. Most casualties respond best when the minimum of treatment is given, and warmth and comfort are still the best medicines for most conditions.

E – EMERGENCY

The last letter of the mnemonic – CHASTE – is also the easiest. All that you have done so far is the action you must take in an accident crisis. It has been an Emergency and you should have treated it as such. There should have been no question of decision by committee; the natural leader should have taken charge and given orders, albeit in a firm but friendly manner. Your actions should have been brisk but calm, you should have been a defusing influence on the situation. Everyone else should have been able to breathe a silent sigh of relief and be glad that X had taken clear charge of the situation. In an Emergency those who make most noise are usually least hurt. The hysterical should be firmly taken out of earshot for the benefit of all. Think of the calm and efficient way that a trained nurse goes about his or her duties and you should emulate this.

Remember 'CHASTE' and you will not go far wrong when faced with a medical emergency be it in a survival situation or otherwise.

OTHER MEDICAL PROBLEMS

So far I have covered the emergency situation but it is likely that, during your survival state and before you return to civilization, you or one of your party will become ill in some way. Shortage of food, lack of proper sleep, cold, damp, etc., will all, because they debilitate the body as a whole, contribute towards possible sickness. For this reason it is important that you take more than the usual care of yourself. A general lassitude will affect most people after a few days and this can lead to inattention when using a knife or other sharp object with obvious results. If your feet are constantly wet and you make no attempt to dry them out you may well succumb to a disease known as 'trench foot'. This odd name originated during the First World War when this was a very common complaint among soldiers who spent long periods standing in trenches, very often deep in mud and water. Some men were crippled for life as a result. Survival is not a time to promote your macho image, but un-

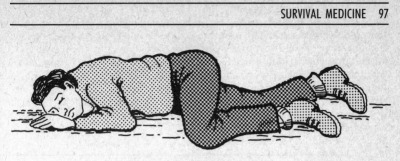

FIG. 76. THE RECOVERY POSITION

ashamedly to give yourself and those with you a lot of tender, loving care of the human frame.

What you can do will vary a lot. At best you will have in your party a doctor or trained medic. Diagnosis of any medical problem should then be fairly easy. What that doctor or medic can do will depend on the resources available and this could range from a very full expedition medical pack complete with a wide range of drugs to nothing more than a dirty handkerchief. As in all survival matters you must do the maximum with the minimum and improvise to the utmost. To give adequate coverage to the treatment of the medical problems likely to be encountered in survival would require most of this volume, but in case you have failed to learn a reasonable amount of first aid and allied medical information the following very brief notes may assist you. The ailments are in no order of priority.

Open Wounds. Remove any obvious foreign bodies and cover with as clean a dressing as possible. If the bleeding is profuse apply the dressing with some pressure. Elevate the limb if applicable.

Cessation of Breathing or Heartbeat. (See page 93).

Unconscious Patient. Provided that the patient is breathing normally and there is a satisfactory pulse, place him in the recovery position (Figure 76) but keep him under close observation by frequent checks. Heart or lungs can cease to function even some time after the initial accident. Treat for shock (see page 95).

Pain. This will occur with varying degrees with most injuries. Time will reduce or eliminate it, but if it is severe the patient should be given suitable pain-killers. Remember that morphine should not be administered if the patient has head injuries or difficulty in breathing.

Eye Injury. Wash with plenty of water. Gently try to remove any foreign bodies but do not persist after the first few attempts.

Fractures and Dislocations. Treat any open wound. Move the patient as little as possible and gently position the limb (if broken) in the most comfortable position for the patient. With broken ribs, collarbone, etc., patient comfort should be the guide as to where and how to apply supporting slings or bandages. Splints can be improvised from branches, rolled up papers, part of a rucksack frame, but if the patient is not comfortable just do not persist with a method just because you have read it in a first-aid book.

Sprains. These could actually be dislocations or fractures masked by swelling so be careful. Normally all that a sprain requires is a bandage (preferably of a crepe-type) and rest.

Burns. Do not try to pull charred clothing away from the burn. Cover it with a clean dressing with plenty of padding. Do not try to renew the dressing at a later stage by pulling it away from the burn. Reduce the pain if it persists and remember that burns can reduce body fluid, so give plenty to drink.

Infection. This can manifest itself in anything from a septic finger to massive infection producing high temperature, delirium and other nasty symptoms. Administer antibiotics if you have any and remember that most of the modern type depend on being used as a five-day course. Do not stop the course just because the infection seems to be clearing up. With an open infection frequent changes of dressing should help by removing pus. Don't tell a dentist this, but I have on a couple of occasions got rid of an abcess under a tooth by wiggling the tooth and biting hard. This seems to break open the abcess and allows it to drain away. This may not be the recommended treatment but it seems to work without any ill effects afterwards.

Cold Injury. This can be anything from slight frostnip to deep frostbite. It is avoidable. Watch yourself and those around you to notice the first whitish spots on the face or hands. Keep thinking about your toes. Can you feel them? If not unlace your boots and warm them in your hands or clothing. Remember to lace boots loosely and have no tight restrictions at the wrist. Under sophisticated conditions it is possible to treat deep frostbite with warm water, but in a survival situation this will probably not be possible. Body heat is the best, either from the casualty himself or his friends. Greater love hath no woman than that she allow her husband to warm his cold feet on her warm stomach!

Heat Injury. Lay the patient down in the shade. If conscious give plenty of liquids with salt (half a teaspoon to a litre) added. If unconscious cool the patient by fanning and saturating his clothing with water. On recovery keep at rest. Sunburn is avoidable. Keep the body covered if there is any risk.

Constipation. This will normally sort itself out in a few days but beware of enforced constipation when it is too cold or too wet or too uncomfortable to go outside. It can also result from people being embarrassed by primitive or no sanitary arrangements.

Diarrhoea. This is normally a symptom of something else, but some people seem to be affected by a change of diet or even water. No food should be given, only liquids to prevent the body becoming dehydrated. Take suitable medication if available.

Blisters. Although minor in themselves they can be critical if your survival depends on walking. At the first sign of a blister or sore place on the foot apply some sort of padding to the area. Adjust the tightness of lacing since this may also cause blisters. Remember your feet can be your passport to safety so look after them.

Carbon Monoxide Poisoning. This can occur in a confined space when using a stove or lamp. Usually there are no symptoms but sometimes, a headache or nausea may give you some warning. If someone collapses get him into fresh air and apply artificial respiration if necessary. Keep a system of ventilation going in any confined space when you are using a stove.

Bugs, various. In the temperate zones of the world none of the ticks, fleas or lice that you may pick up will do you much harm. We just feel it is not nice to have fleas! Check yourself and your clothing. Do not scratch a bite as this brings a risk of infection.

Hypothermia. Caused by a combination of cold and wet conditions. Symptoms are lethargy, slurred speech, stumbling, shivering, pale skin, brief outburst of anger or sudden energy, varying respiration and pulse. Get the casualty into warm and dry conditions and apply body warmth from someone else. Do not assume that apparent recovery is actual recovery. A period of rest is required, normally of some hours.

FIRST-AID KITS

I have deliberately not suggested a list of contents for a first-aid kit. There is no such thing as a standard kit and you should tailor yours to the occasion. The first-aid kit I keep in my car is geared towards road accidents so it has several large dressings suitable for dealing with wounds which are bleeding profusely. It also contains travel sickness tablets suitable for a car journey. The kit I keep in my climbing rucksack still has the dressings but there is no need for travel sickness tablets. When planning the kit for any activity think carefully about the likely risks involved. This will decide some of the contents. Next consider the size of the party. A party of four going off into the hills for a week do not need the sort of kit required by an expedition going to the Himalayas for three months.

Are there any special factors involved? If you are going to a malarial area you must take Paludrine or an equivalent. Have you got to provide medical facilities for local porters, inhabitants, etc.? Is anyone in the party allergic to any of the drugs you have, e.g., penicillin, and should an alternative be provided? How far will you be from sophisticated medical support? If you will never be more than a couple of days from a hospital you will not require a large stock of prescription-type drugs. These are some of the points to bear in mind when planning your first-aid kit. If you are unable to decide what to take your first-aid training is inadequate, and you should not be going on the expedition.

PREVENTIVE ACTION

The human body is both frail and robust. A relatively minor complaint like influenza will make a person feel very unwell and very much reduce his physical ability. His reaction will be to curl up into a tight ball until he has recovered. That same person, when fit, may cover prodigious distances, perform great feats of strength and endure extremes of heat or cold. In a survival situation you are very dependent on the well-being of that human frame be it yours or someone else's. In all walks of life prevention is better than cure so what can you do to minimize the risk of your body breaking down when it most needs to be in perfect working order?

You may be thrown into a survival situation at any time, so you must keep yourself physically and mentally fit as a general mode of life. The real enthusiast will consider every aspect of what he eats, drinks, does, etc., and how it might affect his survival. For the average person, however, let it suffice that he (or she) keep himself reasonably fit and attend to any minor injury or sickness as soon as it occurs. There is no virtue in being a martyr to some ailment which, for the sake of a little time and effort, could be cured. Those who work or take their leisure where there is an enhanced risk of survival action need to think further. It is not wise for the hill-walker to go off to the hills in winter within a few days of apparently recovering from a bad cold. A fisherman on a trawler should not be nursing a torn muscle or ligament. The human machine should always be kept running smoothly and sweetly.

For certain activities you would be wise to take special precautions. For a canoeing holiday on the River Wye you probably need do no more than check that your bouyancy aid is in good order and that you have some plasters for blisters. For a major overseas expedition a medical check before you go would be useful; certain innoculations would be vital. Once in the field you and your party may need to ensure that you drink not one drop of water that has not been purified. A bad dose of Kathmandu Quickstep at 13,000 feet is no laughing matter. You may decide that eating local food uncooked is too much of a risk. In camp, the siting of a latrine area (downwind and downhill) is important. If someone does become ill treat him early. If there is a risk of infection, start the course of antibiotics early not late. In remote areas it is never wrong to use a sledgehammer to crack a nut. A casualty can hinder a party to the point of danger. If you are a leader you must be firm about the treatment of those with you, and you need to keep your eyes on everyone to make sure they are not quietly but irrevocably leading you all into a survival situation.

IMPROVISED REMEDIES

In an ideal situation a sophisticated first-aid kit sufficient to treat any ailment will be available to you. In reality this will seldom be the case and you will have to improvise. Remember that modern medicine is just that – very modern. People have been improvising treatments and cures from natural resources for thousands of years. The following is a miscellany of cures (not all of which I claim to have tried!) culled from prisoner-of-war accounts, old woodcraft-type books and other sources. There are tales of the Old Wild West when men amputated limbs with nothing more than a knife and a sawblade. Only you, in the situation you are in, can decide how far you go with the treatment of a casualty. All I know is that I would rather be alive after some rather unusual treatment than dead waiting for the perfect treatment.

For diarrhoea you can take powdered chalk or charcoal. If you have any bones, burn them and grind them into powder and take it. Strip the bark off a tree (oak is claimed to be best), boil it for at least twelve hours and drink the result. The tannic acid in the brew is the part that cures, so very strong tea can also help and as a by-product it gets fluid, always vital for any diarrhoea case, into the system. If you think you have got worms, two tablespoonfuls of paraffin should cure you.

If you have lice or other 'bugs' you must pick them off yourself, your clothing and other people at least daily.

If you want something sterile for washing wounds, burns, etc., human urine straight from the source is satisfactory. Unpleasant though it may

sound, maggots in a wound do no harm. In fact they do good because they only eat dead tissue and that is a useful thing in the treatment of wounds.

Dressings can be improvised from any sort of absorbant material. Sphagnum moss was collected and dried in large quantities for medical use during the First World War, and gipsy women used to use it as sanitary towels. Slings can be made from any sort of sheeting, cloth, plastic or paper. Splints can be made from anything that provides support, and I have used tree branches, rolled up newspapers, iceaxes and metal tubing.

If you have an abscess or a boil you should use a poultice. Try soft boiled rice wrapped in a cloth applied hot, or a cloth impregnated with soap and with sugar worked into it, also applied hot. If you have no rice try boiled potatoes or oatmeal in a cloth. Finally clay or cow's manure heated and spread over a cloth covering the abscess is claimed to have very good drawing properties.

Stings and bites can be rubbed or covered with a piece of onion or dock leaves. If you need to make someone vomit a good emetic is a lot of salt or dry mustard in lukewarm water.

DEATH

Only a doctor may certify death, but a time may come when, despite your unremitting efforts to apply the 'kiss of life' or other treatments, there is no response. No one sign of possible death should be taken as confirmation of the fact but the following, if mostly present, can be accepted as probably indicating death: no heartbeat or pulse, no misting of a mirror or similar object placed close to the mouth and nose, eyes glazed, pupils dilated and no movement under strong torchlight, body cold and skin remains indented when pressed with the thumb, lips may be blue and the muscles stiff.

If you finally decide that someone is dead you should place the body a little way from the camp. In a temperate climate a body can remain unburied for a few days and this is probably the best course if early rescue is anticipated since if possible the body should be taken back to civilization for proper burial. You may have to protect the body temporarily, by covering it with stones, etc., against interference by animals. In a hot climate burial should take place soon after death, but do remember first to remove the contents of pockets, watches, rings, etc., to return to the next of kin in due course.

If you decide to effect your own rescue by walking out, you must never reduce your own chances of survival by trying to carry a body with you. Bury it and mark the grave clearly so that it can be recovered later.

For the benefit of those remaining, some form of simple service or prayer should be conducted during the burial as a fitting mark of respect. Afterwards the routine of the camp should be quietly re-established as soon as possible to ensure everyone continues their own personal efforts to survive.

9. BOATS AND WATER

The previous chapters of this book have been devoted to survival on land, but since the greater part of the earth is covered by water it would be wrong if it did not deal with the problem of survival in water. Water poses some problems of survival similar to those on land, and some which are very different. The risk of hypothermia in water is as great, if not greater, as on a rain and windswept mountainside. On the other hand, the sources of food at sea are very much less, generally speaking, than those on land. Those readers whose work or leisure involves them only with water must not think that they can ignore the rest of this book. On the contrary, they should read all of it and consider how it applies to their particular environment even in an adapted form. In order to keep this chapter within reasonable limits only inland and coastal waters will be considered; those who venture on Round the World Yacht Races and the like will be presumed to have studied the problems of ocean survival in detail. In keeping with the treatment accorded to the rest of the book, this is not a training manual on 'how to swim' or the specialized lifesaving techniques taught by the relevant societies.

Going on any sort of vessel or aircraft (except as a totally unthinking passenger) involves a deliberate act by choice, and it is probably for this reason that most boat owners, private pilots, etc., take care to provide at least the recommended items of survival equipment in the way of radios, marker flares, lifejackets, etc. Many amateur yachtsmen take a very professional pride in their safety gear and the overall standard of their craft. This is in contrast to those on land who go out for a walk, often in high places, without so much

as a map or compass. The mariner anticipates that the weather could change, his boat could founder, and he caters for such an event as best he can. The landsman sees no hazard in going for a walk; and within reason rightly so, but it is never clear when a walk on the local bit of rough ground with the dog begins to be a walk in more rugged terrain requiring additional knowledge and equipment.

Any safety equipment, from a canoe throwline to a highly sophisticated radio, is only valuable if you know how to use it. It is not like an insurance policy where the mere possession of it covers you against certain risks. The ownership of safety gear does not do likewise. You must know how to use it under all conditions; not just in the comfort of the shop where you buy it, but at night, when you have lost your torch, in appalling weather, when you are dog-tired and probably very frightened. You may not want to fire off a succession of expensive flares, but you can read the instructions until you know them by heart and you can sit, with your eyes closed, and feel the flare all over to determine what it would feel like in the dark and how you would activate it. You would not be popular if you practised with your radio on the emergency frequency, but you can have a dry run with the power off or use a frequency which will not affect anyone. The important thing is to know what buttons to press or knobs to turn.

The person who is only an occasional boat user is probably the person most at risk rather than the man who is a highly enthusiastic canoeist or yachtsman. I am thinking of the man on holiday who hires a boat 'for a bit o' sea fishing' or buys a rubber dinghy 'for the family to have some fun'. No matter how infrequently you use it, no boat can be considered complete without the accepted scale of safety gear.

INLAND WATERS

Most of these are very innocent and under the right conditions offer very little risk, but there is no shortage of rapids and weirs on our rivers and canals. The first thing that any reputable school of instruction or responsible friend will teach a novice is what to do if his boat turns over (capsizes). Only a canoe (of the kayak pattern) poses any real problem and even here the technique of forward rolling out of the upturned boat is soon learned. Do not try to right the canoe, but use it as additional buoyancy and, floating with the stream or current, swim towards the bank. It is easier to hold on to the end of a canoe rather than the centre. Recover your paddle if you can, but do not put yourself at any increased risk. Always stay with the canoe, it is a bigger, brighter object than you, and you will be more easily seen by others. You should know by previous reconnaissance whether there are any hazards ahead. If there are, a time will come when you must abandon your canoe and swim for the side. If you capsize a canoe in rapids, hang on to the upstream end endeavouring to steer it clear of rocks.

A sailing dinghy or similar boat can usually be righted by standing on the keel and pulling on the gunwale, but if this is difficult the correct procedure, as with a canoe, is to stay with the boat because it is a much bigger and more colourful marker than a human being, even one clad in a brightly-coloured lifejacket. If you have capsized a rubber dinghy climb on to one side, reach over for the lifeline on the other side and heave, at the same time pushing down with your feet or knees on the near side. If successful this deposits you back in the water so pull yourself round to one end of the rubber boat and climb in over that end. Figure 77 shows this manoeuvre.

If for some reason you become separated from your boat and cannot reach it – relax. Let your lifejacket or buoyancy aid hold you up and swim slowly towards help. If you find anything that will assist buoyancy use it. If you are not even wearing a lifejacket or buoyancy aid – still relax. Try to float on your back, using one arm to wave and attract attention and shout at the same time. Again swim gently, using any current or flow, towards safety. Discard only boots or shoes and an overcoat or similar garment. Keep the rest of your clothing on, it will help to keep you warm. When resting wrap your body up into a ball; again this helps to retain heat. The exception to this is if you decide to use your clothing to make an improvised buoyancy aid. Trousers are the most suitable for this so take them off, knot the ends of the legs, do up the fly and

FIG. 77. RIGHTING A LIFERAFT

FIG. 78. TROUSERS AS AN IMPROVISED FLOAT

holding the waist firmly and wide open reach up above your head and bring them down smartly (Figure 78) onto the surface of the water. Air will be trapped in the legs and if you now draw in the waist tightly you have a good improvised float. A similar but not so efficient float can be made from a shirt. If wearing a skirt do not take it off but float on your back, pull the skirt up to your waist and out of the water, then pull it down with the hem entering the water first to trap air over your thighs. Long full skirts are best for this technique!

COASTAL WATERS

What follows is applicable, in most cases, to aircraft ditching in the sea, as well as to ships of all sizes. A professional crew should have been fully trained and practised in evacuating passengers should the need arise, but a sensible survivalist is never going to rely totally on someone else. In any ship or aircraft make sure you know where the escape hatches are, where the life-jackets are kept and how they are put on. Remember you might not be able to use the nearest escape route so look for an alternative. Read the escape instructions on your cabin wall or in the pocket of the seat in front of you. Remember that other passengers will not have disciplined themselves, as you have, to reacting quietly and calmly in an emergency. Some may panic, others will think only of themselves. At times you may have to apply the principle of minimum force to restrain some people from impeding the crew in the execution of their duties.

When there is no professional crew you become, in effect, part of the crew even if a fairly amateur member. While the skipper is always in charge you should make sure you know where the emergency equipment is and how it is used. Even the captain of a boat is mortal and could be knocked out at the moment of crisis or washed overboard and you might have to take over. In such vessels no one goes along 'just for the ride'. They must be able to take a reasonable part in manning the ship, and this includes an emergency.

A large craft is only abandoned if it becomes quite clear that everyone will be better off in the emergency facilities, but it is wise to take precautions in good time so as to avoid any last-minute panic. If you are well-prepared before you leave the aircraft or boat your chances of survival are that much better. Fresh water is vital, but food, compass, charts, spare clothing, emergency radio and distress signals all need a place. You or the manufacturer may have prepacked items such as tinned water (or a solar still), emergency rations and a compass, but it is unlikely that charts will be included. If you have a radio do not delay sending a distress signal until the last minute. Ideally, you need to send an accurate position, details of the size, type and name of your craft and the number of people on board. It may be helpful to say that you can use alternate radio frequencies. If time is short the vital information to transmit is 'Mayday' (three times) and your position.

Remember that inflatable liferafts, like lifejackets, should never be inflated until required for use and then only *outside* the aircraft door or the boat's hatchway. I was once on an American service aircraft when for no obvious reason one of the liferafts suddenly inflated itself in the cabin. There was no emergency; it just happened, but it did show what a totally unwieldy thing it was. It seemed to fill the fuselage and we only got it out through the door by deflating it; we would never have got it out otherwise. Ideally you launch on the lee side, but the aircraft doors or the list of the ship may prevent this. Remember that sharp objects such as ball-point pens or stiletto-heeled shoes are a real danger to inflatable craft. Leave them behind. Also remove heavy clothing such as an overcoat, but retain close-fitting items such as anoraks, trousers and light shoes (but not heavy wellingtons); you will need all you have got to keep warm. Try to get into the liferaft dry clad, but if you do go into the water get out of it as soon as possible. In cold water you will soon be chilled through.

Once everyone is in the lifeboat or liferaft, they all have the same survival problems, even if some were originally professional seamen and others amateur sailors. The sea is not man's natural environment even to the most experienced sailor let alone aircraft pilots who, almost to a man, never contemplate the possibility of a ditching, although I did once, and only once, meet a RAF helicopter pilot who deliberately wore boots, puttees, etc., in anticipation of having to walk back from a forced landing. Because the sea is unnatural the numbing shock is likely to be greater than being thrown into a survival situation on land. There is a risk of lapsing into total lethargy when there are urgent matters requiring attention.

Your boat, however big or small, is literally your life. Without it you are almost certainly doomed unless the rescue services find you very quickly. Your first, and continuing concern must be for the well-being of the boat. Is it correctly inflated? Is it leaking? Does it need any repair? Is all the equipment secured? Is there any hazard outside, such as jagged debris? Is the bailer to hand? Has a sea anchor been streamed? As in all survival situations you must apply 110 per cent concentration to the task. Although needing some modification for the sea situation the 'Survival – Immediate Actions' given in Appendix 1 are a good guide to your future efforts. You have got the party clear of danger and either you or someone else has taken charge because even the smallest of vessels needs a skipper. Now look outside your own circle for a moment. If there were others on the ship or aircraft where are they? Look for people in the sea or on other liferafts. Currents are fickle so move quickly to link up with other boats before they drift away. There is strength in numbers in this sort of situation. Looking for other survivors is not just a five-minute effort; it must go on, so appoint your first lookout or watchkeeper. Just as important is the watch for and signalling to rescue services. The largest liferaft is a tiny dot in the sea so a lookout is vital night and day. Everyone does a turn at the job except the sick.

After life-saving first aid has been given the additional need will be an issue of sea-sickness pills. Except on a mirror-calm sea the motion of a lifeboat or raft will make all but the strongest seasick. Vomiting leads to loss of liquid which is very dangerous if water is in short supply so an issue of pills all round should be made.

Warmth and shelter are your next priority. Modern liferafts are fully enclosed and give good shelter, but make everyone wring surplus water from all their clothing? It takes a lot of vital body heat to warm up soaked clothing so reduce the water content. In the temperate zones of the world you are very unlikely to become overheated. You cannot get a fire going so every scrap of heat must come from the survivors' body heat. A dry layer next to the skin is the aim, with damp layers over that being dried by the general warmth generated. Make sure the hatch is kept shut and that everyone is insulated as far as possible from the cold sea water. You will never heat up the ocean! In due course food will provide heat to the body, but if this is limited wait until any sea-sickness has been overcome.

Allocate jobs. Someone must control the available food, another should apply himself to water provision, a log or diary writer is important. Any responsibility does wonders for morale and keeps people occupied. You cannot move about much in a lifeboat, not even a few yards away for a 'bit of peace and quiet'. Tempers will fray, hates will develop. Activities and jobs will go some way to coping with these interpersonal problems.

Signalling is paramount. You must use every means possible to attract attention to your situation. Every signalling device you have or can improvise must be brought into play. If you have a radio, use it but remember that its batteries have a finite life. Emergency beacons also have a limited life and if you have both it is probably best to use only one at a time. For visual signals the flashing mirror is probably the best, as it is on land. Marker dyes and smokeflares are best used when you have been spotted and an aircraft or ship needs to turn and come back to find you again. Remember neither can turn 'on a sixpence' and they virtually have to search for you again on their second approach. If you can rig a mast with some sort of radar reflector this can help. Despite your efforts you may not be seen and rescued by the first or even subsequent ships that pass. Not every lookout has perfect vision or dedicated attention to duty. Be mentally prepared for this sort of disappointment.

Water will be more of a problem than on land, but you are likely to have less need of it. You will not be out hunting for food, looking for fuel, etc. Much of your time will be spent sitting still. The liferaft equipment may contain desalting tablets or a solar still and these should be used in preference to any bottled or tinned water. Be ready to catch every drop of rainwater by rigging sheeting, sails, etc., to channel the water into containers. Look back at the chapter on 'Water' to see how to work out a sensible rationing scheme. Even when you appear to have plenty you should continue the scheme, albeit with a revised ration. Only when every possible container is full and you are still collecting rainwater can you feel free to drink your fill. Under no circumstances should you drink seawater (even mixed with fresh), urine, alcohol or bird's blood. Smoking increases thirst and

protein foods such as meat need an increase of water intake to digest. Your watchkeeper should keep his eyes open for the approach of rain clouds and be ready to catch the rain when it falls. If it rains take the opportunity to have a shower or wash in fresh water to remove salt from your skin. Old sea ice, which is blue and wellrounded will be salt free and can be melted for fresh water. Much more than on land your efforts must be directed to reducing your body's need for water. You cannot help losing about 2 pints per day; your aim must be to lose not a single drop more. A bead of sweat is a drop of water wasted.

Your ability to fix your position will depend on your knowledge of navigation and the equipment you have with you. If you are an offshore sailor you should be able to continue navigating as if you were in your original boat since you should have taken charts and other aids with you when you abandoned ship. If you are a passive passenger from an aircraft ditching you may not be able to do very much and are unlikely to have navigational equipment. Between these two extremes there is infinite variety. What you should appreciate is that you will almost certainly move in some direction due to the ocean currents. Initially you should try to remain in the area of your ditching. This is the location you gave in your distress signal and that is where rescue services will search first. If you are aware of the currents that affect that area it is worth making efforts to keep yourself as static as possible. A traditional lifeboat can be rowed, but the average rubber liferaft is a singularly unmanageable beast if it is round and only marginally better if it is not.

Ultimately you must decide if you are going to stay put as best you can or try to move. The currents and the prevailing winds will probably make the decision for you to a large extent, but by careful trimming of a sail or a certain amount of paddling you may be able to modify drift. Obviously your aim is to reach land or get into the busy shipping lanes. Make a very conservative estimate as to the time it may take to reach help if only to give a guide to food rationing. Unless you can navigate accurately you should aim to hit a long coastline rather than an isolated landfall such as a small island. An increase in the number of birds seen is an indication of approaching land and you should note the general direction of their flight. Many will be coming to the sea to catch food and then returning to land. Drifting vegetation is another useful indicator as is fixed cloud which will indicate high ground on the land. Once land has been sighted, every effort, by sailing, rowing, paddling and anything else you can think of, must be made to reach it. Then your problems of land survival may begin!

Food sources at sea are likely to be more limited than on land, but this is not always so. On a recent expedition to Greenland, someone had only to sit out in the fjord in a boat for half an hour and hang a few lines over the side to catch almost any number of fish and large, succulent arctic char at that. A fish diet may not be everyone's choice, but it is a nourishing one. At sea, apart from any survival rations in your liferaft, you will be dependent on fish and perhaps birds. Because they are packed for long storage you should always eat your survival rations as a last resort.

Fresh food will not keep for very long. In temperate zones all fish are safe to eat. Just clean out the entrails. Do not rely on one method of fishing, try casting from the boat as well as dropping lines over the side. If you catch more fish than you can consume, clean them and cut the flesh into strips and dry it for consumption in leaner days to come. Try anything as bait. Fish may be attracted by even such things as a sliver of silver paper from a cigarette packet or a tiny piece of coloured cloth. Do remember, however, that fish are protein and need a reasonable availability of water. If water is very short it is better to go hungry. You can survive quite well for weeks without food, but you cannot afford to squander limited supplies of water by using it to digest protein foods.

The sea or any large stretch of water with no land in sight poses its own psychological problems. It will never seem as friendly as land because man is a land animal. The constant motion, the close proximity of a lot of people in a liferaft, the constant wetness will all tax survivors to the utmost, but you can survive. Poon Lim, a Chinese sailor who was on a ship torpedoed during the Second World War, survived for 133 days and was in quite good shape when rescued. Most of the contents of this book apply as much to sea as to land survival. The ideas and methods may need modification but the principles apply.

10. WHEN NATURE STRIKES: Natural hazards

Survival is usually considered against the natural elements as they exist. These elements may vary from extreme heat to extreme cold, from bare mountain rock to impenetrable jungle, but they are 'as found' in the world as it is. Sometimes Nature goes to the limit and produces flood, fire, earthquakes and the like; what insurers usually call 'Acts of God'. This chapter will consider briefly the special survival problems associated with these natural disasters. Each could justify a book of its own, but a few guiding hints may be useful since your basic survival situation could be compounded by one of these additional natural hazards.

AVALANCHE

These can happen even in the modest hills of Scotland and are not limited to major mountain ranges. Seldom a winter passes without at least one accident involving an avalanche. The causes are numerous; being an interaction between the weather, angle of slope, type of snow, its degree of metamorphosis and other factors, even to the disturbance caused by the tracks of a skier. No walker, skier or climber should be on the winter hills unless he has some knowledge of avalanches and the conditions under which they are likely to occur. The survivor who does not have this knowledge should note the following precautions. In warm weather avoid traversing below cornices (the overhanging curl of snow and ice often seen on a ridge or at the top of a steep slope) (Figure 41), steep slopes and gullies, especially if there has been a recent fall of new snow (within the last 24/48 hours). If an avalanche does occur avoid it if you can by rushing for the nearest bit of higher ground, shedding your rucksack at the same time. If you are enveloped keep your mouth shut and make a swimming motion with your arms and legs. Ideally this should be towards the surface if your are not totally disorientated. As the movement slows bring your arms around your face to form an air pocket in which you can breathe comfortably. Just before all movement stops make as massive an effort as you can to keep your body loose in the snow. Once everything has stopped, keep calm and try to decide which way up you are. Once you have decided this try to move towards the surface, although this will often not be possible. Shout for help but not continuously or you will soon run out of voice and effort. If you are not caught in the avalanche yourself, but someone else is, try to note the last point at which he was visible and then follow his likely path at the rate at which the avalanche is moving. When it stops note where you think he might have got to and start your search there.

FLOOD

In temperate zones of the world you are unlikely to be suddenly caught in a flood. Rivers may rise rapidly but not instantaneously. The obvious thing to do is get higher, either to an upper floor in a building or to higher ground. This is what might be termed a controlled survival situation, where you can take some precautions before the situation actually happens. Before retreating to your upper floor think what you will need for a prolonged stay. You will want warmth with extra clothing, blankets, etc. You will want water, food and a means of cooking it. A couple of books or children's games would not go amiss if you have a young family. A bucket as an improvised lavatory would be useful plus any of the other items you might take on a camping holiday because that is, in effect, what you are going to do – camp in your bedroom.

FIRE

This can be from natural causes or as the result of a man-made error. Make one quick attempt to put the fire out. If this fails get out of the building, closing doors and windows as you go. Raise the alarm and keep well out of the way of the fire and the fire brigade. If caught out in a forest or similar fire, head either for open country or, if the fire is moving faster than you can run, find a river, pool or other patch of water and get in it. Even in open country you should keep close to water because a moorland fire, fanned by a strong wind, can move very rapidly. Bare rocky ground, which offers no potential fuel for the blaze, is another place to head for. Wet clothing is an aid to survival in a fire so do not be afraid to jump in a river. Note the direction of the wind and therefore the fire and move out of its path. If you have a fire from a stove in a tent, kick or throw the stove outside. Do not try to put the fire out. You will only lose your tent which may be vital to your survival.

BLIZZARDS

If caught in a blizzard your first priority is shelter. In winter you should be aware of your nearest refuge if your work or play takes you out into rugged conditions. The combination of wind, cold and driving snow can be very energy-sapping and you should beware of pressing on if your party is not as strong as you are. A time may well come when a hastily dug snow trench is better for your party than pressing on to a better refuge. It is very much a question of judgement. During the winter you might well keep a sleeping-bag, shovel, emergency food, towrope, etc., in your

car especially if your travels take you over exposed roads or through sparsely inhabited areas.

LIGHTNING

Thunder gives a good audible warning and lightning a good visual warning of the risk. If caught in the open do not do the obvious thing which is to seek shelter under trees, boulders, etc. Keep off exposed mountain tops and ridges. If you want to stop do so on a slope and make yourself as small as possible. Sit on your rucksack or on a dry rope to minimize your contact with the ground. But there is no special value in stopping. A building, car or flat ground offer the safest places. A person struck by lightning is not always killed, but will usually need first aid so treat him as a normal first aid casualty. Do not discard your iceaxe if you have one, you may need it later.

ANIMALS

Animals can be a hazard; people do get gored by bulls and bitten by snakes but so infrequently that virtually every occurrence is media news. Newcomers to the jungle are struck by the apparent lack of animals. Probably the major risk, worldwide, is where man has done something which attracts wild animals. An obvious example is campsites in America where campers have attractive food which brings bears and other animals to investigate. It is at times like this that animal/man accidents happen. If face to face with an animal do nothing to frighten or antagonize it. Back quietly away. If the animal follows, discard an object or a garment; it will usually stop to investigate. With some animals you can climb a tree as a refuge. Tree-climbing bulls have yet to be invented, but bears like to climb trees. Some animals do not like water so a nearby river could be a haven. Never hold out a hand to a doubtful animal even a dog which is not known. A long hard look such as a duchess might give a recalcitrant second footman may have the desired effect. If actually entangled with an animal fight as dirty as you like; shout and scream, and aim to hurt tender parts of the animal.

11. CIVILIZATION IS A DANGEROUS PLACE: Man-made hazards

Survival is usually thought of as something which happens in an emergency miles from anywhere in bad weather, but our allegedly civilized society of the late twentieth century is not without its hazards. This chapter offers a few hints on just some of the possible survival situations you may meet, probably in places where you least expect them. The situations are in no particular order of importance.

CAR CRASH

Whether it is your own crash or someone else's makes little difference except that if you have been involved you will soon begin to suffer some degree of shock. First, you should make a very quick assessment as to the hazard caused by the crash to other traffic. If the crash is on a bend or not obvious to approaching vehicles, send someone out to wave them down. An uninvolved vehicle with its hazard warning lights flashing positioned in front of the crash is very useful. The next quick decision required is should you remove any injured persons from the crash vehicles? If there is a smell of petrol it is probably wise to do so, but remember they may have serious injuries to back or neck which need very careful handling if you are to avoid increasing the damage. In any case it is worth turning the ignition off. C-H-A-S-T-E should now be your guide. When you get to 'A for Aid' make sure the person going for help realizes that he needs the nearest telephone which, except on a motorway, will usually be in a private house. He must not go for miles looking for a public call-box. At a private house he may have to be quite forceful about using the telephone and must not be put off by an unhelpful householder.

Emergency calls are free so there is no need for coins. Once the police and other services arrive let them take over.

CAR BREAKDOWN

Normally this is just an annoyance, but at times it can involve a survival decision. A few months before writing this book I was driving over the mountain road from Machynlleth to Llanidloes in Central Wales. It was March and the weather at sea level was mild. Near the top of the road at about 400 metres I found snow on the road and was thinking of turning back when the car stuck in a small snowdrift. I reversed out and decided to back down the hill only to find that I had just come over a rise which was now too thick with snow to back the car up. I was stuck in a dip between two quite minor slopes, but they were sufficient to prevent a two-wheel drive vehicle going either way. I had a sleeping-bag, shovel, food and a flask and was well clad. Should I stay or should I walk back the way I had come? It was snowing, but the depth was not enough for me to miss the road and wander off across the moors. About half a mile back was the last house up that road and thereafter there were cottages or houses no more than about half a mile apart. Weighing up all these factors I decided it was worth walking back and that it was safe for me, as a reasonably fit outdoor person, to do so. It would not have been the right decision for a young mother with two toddlers. If your car breaks down do, before you start getting involved with fault-finding, give a quick thought to the question of survival. It could be better to leave the car and get out while you can, or perhaps allow yourself ten minutes and if you have not started it by then, take the decision to go. This book is not the place for a course in car mechanics, but a modest knowledge of fault-finding is very useful, as is membership of one of the motoring organizations!

FIRE

See Chapter Ten.

AIRCRAFT CRASH

The procedures to be followed if you are in crashed or ditched aircraft have been covered earlier in this book, but what happens if you see an aircraft make a forced landing and you arrive on the scene shortly afterwards? The first rule is to keep well away from both ends of jet engines, and from propellers. Unless the fuselage breaks open on impact an aircraft is effectively a sealed metal cylinder and you have got to gain entry. Look around the aircraft and you will find signs indicating that by pulling, pushing, twisting or turning something you can get in. Also note that there may be additional warning signs telling you to keep clear in certain areas. If the aircraft is a military one, in addition to the hazard from engines, it may be armed with rockets, bombs or ammunition, which can also offer a risk and should be avoided. In fast jet military aircraft the crew will sit in ejector seats and these must be made safe before you do anything else. Usually this is done by inserting a split safety-pin, normally labelled with a large red label or tag, into a hole on the top of the seat. Having gained entry you carry out the first aid sequence and alert the emergency services, just as you would with a car crash. The difference is that you may have many more casualties than in a car accident. The sheer numbers will appear overwhelming at first, but if you deal only with the real killers of lungs and heart not functioning and severe bleeding you will not go far wrong. Because of the numbers you must con-

centrate in getting others to do things. Even someone who is slightly injured himself can apply pressure hard to a handkerchief held to a major wound on somebody else.

MAN OVERBOARD

This is not an infrequent event and it is a drill which should be practised before it is needed in real life. If someone falls overboard announce the fact as loudly as possible. Everyone should then keep their eyes on the person in the water because even in good weather the easiest thing to do is to lose sight of a person in a large expanse of water. Whether you are under sail or power it takes time to bring a vessel round onto the reverse course and it is during this turn of 180° that someone can be lost from view. Despite the urgency of the situation the man in the water must be approached slowly. Especially under sail, it is possible to overshoot and the turning process has to be repeated. As the approach is made, a lifebuoy on a line should be got ready and looped lines put over the side. If he is in the water for more than a very few minutes he will need a lot of help to get him on board again. A ladder over the side will also assist. Once on board, dry clothing and warm surroundings are the priority followed by a hot drink. Alcohol in any form, as in all hypothermia cases, should be avoided. It hinders rather than assists recovery despite its apparent warming effect.

ELECTROCUTION

The first requirement is to cut off the current by turning off the switch, pulling out the plug, turning off at the mains, etc. If this is impossible, push or pull the casualty away from the source of power with a *dry* object which does not conduct electricity. Assume that any metal object will conduct current so avoid these. Wood, rubber, paper, etc., provided that they are dry do not. Most likely first aid requirement will be to restart the casualty's breathing.

GAS HAZARD

Anyone who has collapsed in a room with a gas appliance in it should be removed from the room and resuscitated with the 'kiss of life'. If you suspect a gas escape, remove everyone from the scene, call the local gas authority and try to turn off the gas at the main supply. Carbon monoxide is produced by most processes of burning. It is colourless and odourless so is difficult to detect. It is very common from the exhaust fumes of a car or burning a stove in a confined space. Get any collapsed casualty into fresh air and resuscitate him.

TRAIN CRASH

The safest position in a train is a seat with your back to the engine. If a crash occurs it will be similar to an aircraft crash with possibly many casualties. As with a road crash there may be a risk to a following train, or one on the other line if the crash has blocked it. Try to find out from train staff if this is likely, but do not delay too long before going up or down the line to give a warning. Remember that trains need a long distance to slow up – hundreds of metres – so go a long way. Telephones can be found on some lines at intervals beside the track.

HUMAN ATTACK

These can range from a belligerent but unsteady drunk to a determined, if mentally unbalanced, terrorist. Unless you are trained and *experienced* in one of the forms of unarmed combat, discretion is the better part of valour, and you try to fade quietly from the scene. Talking can delay an attacker and allow you time to edge nearer to an escape route or a possible weapon. Screaming or shouting may raise the alarm and could discourage your attacker. Try to avoid getting within the grasp of an attacker, but if you do then anything goes. Use any sharp object you have, kick, bite, pull hair, etc. Go for the face, genitals and other tender parts of the body. As soon as you can, break away and run, remembering to kick your shoes off if you are wearing high heels. With a bunch of hijackers in the confined space of an aircraft things are more serious. They are likely to believe in a cause and be less concerned about ultimate death than the average cowardly attacker. The key thing is to keep cool, calm and not to draw attention to yourself. Slump in your seat and remind yourself where the escape hatches are should you need them. Make no sudden movements. Quietly get rid of any documents or literature which might antagonize the hijackers. Currently this is anything American or Israeli, but could change in the future according to the political views of the hijackers. Demand nothing, offer nothing. Reasoning or discussion of their alleged cause is unlikely to assist the situation. Rest, sleep and generally husband your physical and mental resources for the time when they may be needed which will come, inevitably, sooner or later.

APPENDIX 1. Survival – Immediate Actions

1. Remove persons from immediate danger. Get them clear of water, avalanche, etc.
2. Render first aid. See below for priority order.
3. Stop, think and plan.
4. Start providing shelter – from wind, wet and cold.
5. Allocate jobs.
6. Put out markers, signalling devices, etc.
7. Find water and fuel.
8. Fix your position as accurately as possible.
9. Decide if, and when, you will send for help.
10. Continue all the above until found.

Remember the keyword – CHASTE.

C – Choking/Cardiac. Get the casualty breathing and his heart beating as quickly as possible.
H – Haemorrhage. Stop major bleeding. Ignore minor cuts.
A – Aid. Get others to help you and, if possible, send for an ambulance.
S – Shock. Treat in the normal way.
T – Treatment. Deal with other injuries, e.g., fractures, burns, etc.
E – Emergency. The situation is one, so deal with it quickly and firmly.

APPENDIX 2. Survival Kits

These are available for various purposes from a number of firms. Their failing is that their contents have to be fairly general in order to cater for a wide market. Survival kits are also to be found on virtually all aircraft, both military and civil and in lifeboats and liferafts. Neither I nor anyone else can decide what you need for the activities you undertake, except by individual discussion with you. I have listed the contents of a very wide range of survival kits. The aim is to jog your memory as to what you might select for yourself. To take all the items listed would require a vehicle just to carry them and there is no suggestion that you should select more than a small number of items. The makeup of any kit is a compromise between what you think you might need and what you can carry or pack. Beware of the kitchen sink attitude and be ruthless in your selection.

Some of the items may appear to duplicate one another or nearly so. Obviously a groundsheet and a poncho could be the same item but they have come from different lists. The items have been grouped under broad headings such as signalling, medical, etc., and a few items appear more than once, e.g., cotton wool has an obvious medical use and can also be used for tinder when lighting a fire. An item like string is so universal that it could appear under most of the headings. Having selected your personal kit you should pack it in a waterproof container and hope that you never have to use it.

Clothing and Shelter
Groundsheet
String
Survival bag
Nylon cord
Space blanket (metalized plastic sheet)
Plastic sheet
Poncho
Half parachute
Sleeping-bag
Woollen hat
Sun hat
Plastic coat and hat
Hammock
Spare socks
Anti-exposure suit
Gloves
Mosquito veil

Signalling
Whistle
Distress flares
Mini flares
Sea marker dye
Torch
Signalling mirror
Distress rockets
Smoke flares
Radio beacon
Ground signals code

Navigation
Compass
Watch
Map

Medical
Chalk
Plasters
Paludrine
Anti-glare shields
Insect repellent
Snakebite kit
Lipsalve
Cotton wool
First-aid kit
Sunglasses
Glacier cream
Shark repellent
Adhesive tape

Firemaking
Matches (waterproof)
Candle
Flint and steel
Lighter
Solid fuel blocks
Cotton wool
Magnifying glass
Firemaking tablets
Small bottle petrol
Liquid fuel stove

Tools
Razor blade
Penknife
Nylon cord
Clasp-knife
Survival knife
Scalpel blade
Wire saw
String
Needle and thread
Oilstone
Pliers
Stout knife
Hacksaw blade
Wire
Nailfile
Sewing kit
Six-inch file
Machete

Obtaining and Preparing Food and Water
Fishing line
Water-purifying tablets
Polythene bag ⎫
Balloon   ⎬ for carrying water
Contraceptive ⎭
Spatula
Water-carrier
Solar still
Fishing kit
Tin-opener
Fish-hooks
Potassium permanganate crystals
Gill net

Wire snares
Spoon
Cooking utensil
Weapon and ammunition
Desalting kit
Plastic cup

Sea Survival
Liferaft
Bailer
Bellows
Sea marker dye
Solar still
Leakstoppers
Sponge
Lifejacket
Radio beacon
Desalting kit

Miscellaneous
Candle
Wire
Pencil
Sponge
Toilet paper
Rucksack
Chemical lights
Watch
Notebook
Survival book
Rubber bands

Suggested Items to be Carried in a Car
Blanket
Emergency food (chocolate, nuts, biscuits, etc.)
First-aid kit
Spare clothing
Tools
Torch
Spare bulbs, fanbelt, etc.
Container of water
Shovel
Jump-leads
Tow rope
Sacking

APPENDIX 3. Emergency Foods

Emergency foods must be light in weight, provide energy rather than protein, edible without cooking, have a long shelf life and be reasonably palatable – but not too palatable or the temptation to consume them other than in an emergency will be too great! The range of possible foods is considerable and frequently changing according to the whim of the food trade. A walk round any large food store will provide plenty of ideas. The following items have all been suggested in the past as good for emergency use.

Dextrose tablets
Lemonade powder
Drinking chocolate
Mint cake
Sugar
Porridge oats
Cheese
Nuts
Margarine
Glucose sweets
Salt tablets
Chocolate
Sweet biscuits
Dehydrated meat blocks
Oatmeal blocks
Milk powder
Tea/Coffee
Dried meat and rice
OXO cubes

In addition, specially prepared survival rations are available commercially.

APPENDIX 4. Survival Training Activities

This book should be used as a training guide and manual. For those, especially youth leaders concerned with the training of young people, who want a quick 'ideas list' the following should provide plenty of programme material.

1. Produce a fire with the aid of a lens, e.g., from binoculars.
2. Produce fire with the aid of a natural flint and a metal object such as a knife blade.
3. Waterproof some matches.
4. Produce fire with the aid of a spark from a vehicle's or similar battery.
5. Improvise a Benghazi Burner.
6. Improvise a wick and use paraffin or oil as fuel.
7. Construct a shelter using natural materials, and spend a night in it.
8. Dig a snowhole or snow trench and spend a night in it.
9. Experiment with a solar still.
10. Cook an animal, fish or bird by improvised means.
11. Try some of the natural foods suggested in Chapter Seven.
12. Select the contents of a first-aid kit for a specific type of activity.
13. Select the contents of a survival kit for a specific type of activity.
14. Hold a discussion group on the mental and physical problems of survival.
15. Improvise and use fishhooks.
16. Improvise snares (but do not leave them out as a risk to animals).
17. Compare cooking over a candle enclosed in a tin with one not so enclosed.
18. Improvise a signalling mirror.
19. Produce a survival fishing kit and test it.
20. Make and use a hammock.
21. Improvise a water filter.
22. Test the various methods of finding north and compare the results with a compass.
23. Test dried animal dung as a fuel.
24. Improvise a raft from natural materials.
25. Try making a coat or other garment from sacking or similar material.
26. Practise, and practise again and again your ability to navigate across country in all weathers.
27. Make and use a flinthead axe.
28. Learn to swim if you cannot already do so.
29. Take a first-aid course.
30. Improvise footwear from old tyres, canvas, etc.
31. Practice the use of an improvised lifejacket, e.g., knotted trousers.
32. Learn how to right a capsized canoe, sailing dinghy, etc.
33. Learn how to cross rivers safely.
34. Learn to abseil safely.
35. Learn how a car works and a simple fault-finding procedure.

SELECTED BIBLIOGRAPHY

The following books, among others, have influenced my thinking, and practise in survival over the last twenty years or more. Some were published many years ago – at least one very early in this century – but survival is not a new science; man has been practising it since long before the invention of printing. In addition the world is full of examples of things which were invented, forgotten, and have had to be reinvented years later. Many of the books are now out of print, but should be available by special request from a public library. Some organizations, such as government departments and airlines, publish books for the benefit of their own staff, but these are not available to the general public and have been omitted from the following list which is confined to publications that are or have been available commercially.

Adam, Lieutenant-Colonel J. M. *A Traveller's Guide to Health*. For The Royal Geographical Society, Hodder & Stoughton

Blackshaw, Alan. *Mountaineering*. Penguin

Byrd, Rear-Admiral R. E. *Alone*. Putnam & Sons

Chapman, F. S. *The Jungle is Neutral*. Chatto & Windus

Cherry-Garrard, Apsley. *The Worst Journey in the World*. Chatto & Windus, now a Penguin

Cliff, Peter. *Mountain Navigation*. Cordee

Craighead, F. C. and Craighead, J. J. *How to Survive on Land and Sea*. Naval Institute Press

Edholm, O. G. and Bacharach, A. L. *Exploration Medicine*. Wright & Sons

——. *Physiology of Human Survival*. London, Academic Press

Farrar-Hockley, General Sir Anthony. *Edge of the Sword*. Frederick Muller

Greenbank, Anthony. *The Book of Survival*. Wolfe Publishing Ltd.

Grenfell, Sir Wilfred. *A Labrador Doctor*. Hodder & Stoughton

Kane, E. Kent. *Arctic Explorations*. Nelson & Sons

Kephart, Horace. *Camping and Woodcraft*. New York, Macmillan

Klaben, Helen. *Hey, I'm Alive*. Hodder & Stoughton

Lindsay, Martin. *Sledge*. Cassell

Mabey, Richard. *Food for Free*. Collins

Mawson, Sir Douglas. *The Home of the Blizzard*. Hodder & Stoughton

Mikkalsen, Ejnar. *Two Against the Ice*. Hart Davis

Moran, Lord. *The Anatomy of Courage*. Constable & Co.

Nansen, Fridtjof. *First Crossing of Greenland*. Longmans Green

Nesbit, P. H., Pond, A. W. and Allen, W. H. *The Survival Book*. van Nostrand

Nicholl, G. W. R. *Survival at Sea*. Adlard Coles

Noyce, Wilfred. *They Survived*. Heinemann

Rodahl, Kaare. *North*. New York, Harper

Scott, J. M. *Gino Watkins*. Hodder & Stoughton

Shackleton, Sir Ernest. *South*. Macmillan

Stefansson, Vilhjalmur. *The Friendly Arctic*. New York, Macmillan

Langmuir, Eric. *Mountaincraft and Leadership*. Scottish Sports Council and Mountainwalking Leader Training Board

Mountain Rescue. HMSO

Safety on Mountains. British Mountaineering Council

Survival pamphlets on Arctic, jungle, desert and sea survival, Ministry of Defence, reprint. Survival Aids Ltd.

Troebst, C. C. *The Art of Survival.* W. H. Allen

Wiseman, John. *The SAS Survival Handbook.* Collins Harvill

INDEX

79, 86, 88